A Sunset Book

HOW TO MAKE

POTTERY &
Ceramic Sculpture

Herbert H. Sanders, Ph. D.
Professor of Ceramic Art, San José State College

Doris Aller
Consulting Editor, Sunset Craft Books

LANE BOOKS, MENLO PARK, CALIFORNIA

Cover photos, starting at top and reading clockwise: Slab vase with coil-built neck; combined pinch-formed teapot. Paddled vase with black glaze applied over ground of white matt glaze. Decorative tile panels mounted on wood. Globular bottle with matt glaze; wine pot with black gloss glaze. Glazed decorative tile panel. Demonstration of (left) attaching a pulled spout on a thrown pitcher, and (right) decorating a bowl with painted slip.

Library of Congress Catalog Card Number 64-22657. Title Number 410.

Eleventh Printing July 1972

ACKNOWLEDGMENTS

The author wishes to acknowledge his gratitude to the many students and friends who contributed to this book, chiefly Harold Driscoll, Paula Palmer, Doris Aller, and F. Carlton Ball, all through photographs previously published in Sunset Magazine.

Many students of San Jose State College, as well as professors of ceramics, contributed examples of completed ware: Ruthadell Horan, Ruth Spoon, Kay Salazar, Elliott House, Gene Kenefick, George Eimers, Dennison Herring, Betty Locke, Marvin Wax, Gary Peters, Cecile McCann, Joan Bugbee, Maryann Gravitt, Jan Jones, Warren Westerberg, Elias Arenas, Fred W. K. Hamilton, Claude Horan, Tom Fredricks, Charles Abrahams, Gary Boero, Theresa Fye, Bill Grossi, Gene Chappell, Larry Geremone, Carol Hales, Mario, Arthur Baggs, and Frances Cochran. Special thanks go to Ernie Kim for the lamp on page 9, Louise Pfeiffer for work at top of page 31, and Kenneth Dierck, who designed and made the tiles on page 43. The following students provided glaze compositions: Cecile McCann, Trent Thompson, Bob Noll, Nancy Lynch, Jan Jones, Robert Smith, Warren Westerberg, Mary Auvil, Joan Bugbee, and Fred Lucero. Pat and Bruce Bangert appear in the cover photograph. Throughout the book, the names that appear with photos are of the artist. Finished pieces not credited are, in most cases, by the author.

Process-sequence photos were provided by Gene Kenefick, Joseph L. Hysong, Maryann Gravitt, Philip Cornelius, Joseph Hawley, Jan Jones, Doris Aller, Professor Claude Horan, John Leary, James Lovera, and Robert Fritz. The following photographers took most of the new sequence pictures: Robert Fritz, Gene Kenefick, Claude Horan, Joseph M. Campbell, Charles Mulkey, Fred W. K. Hamilton, Wes Hammond, and Marvin Wax. Ernie Kim's lamp was photographed by Associated Press, Mrs. Aller's work by her husband, Paul Aller, Mrs. Palmer's by her husband, Phil Palmer. The photo of the Indian urn is by courtesy of the Museum of the American Indian, Heye Foundation, New York City.

FOREWORD

Clay is a basic craft medium and the making of pottery one of our most popular crafts. It is undoubtedly the kindly and gentle nature of the medium which accounts for much of the popularity of the craft—soft, moist clay, plastic and pliable, is so easily formed into sturdy pottery pieces. The satisfying results to be achieved through the most elementary effort make clay an ideal medium for those who seek a craft activity for relaxation during leisure hours, as well as for those who will use it for educative or therapeutic purposes.

This book describes the methods and materials used to make pottery by hand processes. It is intended as a manual of self-instruction for the beginner who will work at home, as supplementary material for both student and teacher in the classroom, and for use in the work of therapy and rehabilitation done in community centers and hospitals.

Although parts of this book will interest potters at any stage of achievement and experience, it is intended for the complete novice. First steps are planned and presented to accord with developing abilities. Later steps, although not often undertaken by the beginner working alone, will provide an understanding of all the phases of the craft and permit him to make a better beginning in it.

CONTENTS

Stoneware coffee urn. Stained stoneware
body, unglazed outside.

Earthenware chocolate set. Mottled silver and gray glaze, violet and green reflections.

1 · Ceramics as a Hobby

The craft of pottery making is being enthusiastically accepted by those people who seek a pleasurable recreational activity, by those who would add to their knowledge and skills in handicrafts, and by those who use crafts as a tool in teaching or therapy. Working with clay appeals to all these people, because the pliant, responsive material allows for achievement in some phase of the craft regardless of the degree of skill or ability of the worker.

Modern schools provide even the youngest pupils with soft clay for their creative play. As play material, the plastic properties of clay can be exploited without thought of an end product—the pleasure in pinching and pushing the clay into various forms is sufficient. As a craft material, clay is shaped and put through the various processes needed to make it a finished, usable piece.

You discovered that shaping a plastic mixture of earth and water was fun when you made your first mud pie. You took your materials as, and where, you found them and your product was "baked" by an obliging sun. In a sense, your mud pie experience was your initial introduction to ceramics.

The term "ceramic" properly applies to a vast number of products made by shaping moist clay, or similar substances, which are then dried and subjected to temperatures high enough to give the finished article strength and permanence. Ceramic products therefore include bricks, sewer tile, porcelain fittings, to name but a few. From this it will be seen that the craft of making pottery bowls, plates and such pieces by hand occupies but a small corner in the broad field of ceramics. There is room in it, however, for unlimited experiment and achievement for the craftsman, whether beginner or experienced potter.

This book is meant, first of all, for the novice who would like to try his hand at pottery making without acquiring expensive tools or equipment. It is quite possible to test the depth of your interest with a few pounds of moist pottery clay, a very few tools and little equipment. You can be assured, too, that your very first efforts toward making things by hand with clay can be successful and satisfying. As in the practice of any craft, learning will come with doing. With each piece you make you will learn more about handling clay, and with each method you use you'll better appreciate the value of ceramics as a gratifying hobby.

The first factor of importance in the practice of any hobby is its basic raw material. In pottery this is clay. Clay is plentiful and inexpensive. You can buy it as dry powder and mix it with water, or you can buy it moist and ready for use. Clay is clean and easy to handle. It doesn't deteriorate, is easy to care for and store. If it becomes too dry to work, water will make it soft and pliable again; and spills and splashes can be wiped up with a water-dampened sponge. Clay can be reconditioned and reworked indefinitely until it has been fired.

The hands and fingers are the main "tools" used by the potter, regardless of the shaping method he uses. Direct handling of the material is especially desirable for the beginner as a method of "getting acquainted." The few essential tools and minimum equipment needs for use in any of the hand-building methods are listed in the following chapter.

Each pottery piece, however formed, must undergo certain kinds of treatment and phases of handling before it is a finished product. A little advance knowledge of these somewhat interlocked processes will be of benefit whether or not you choose to undertake them all in the making of your first pieces.

In reading the following brief descriptions of ceramic processes, note the words which are a part of the special vocabulary of pottery work. At some time in the craft's long history these words and phrases may have been a part of the everyday language. Now they have specific meanings rather than general ones.

As a starting example, the potter refers to all clay pieces in the making, with the exception of sculptures, as "pots" and of his operations in making these as "potting." Pots formed on the potter's wheel are spoken of as "thrown" and the work of making them as "throwing."

Before a mass of clay is used to make any piece, either hand-built or wheel-thrown, it is first cut, smacked and slapped in a vigorous manner to expel any air bubbles and to bring it to an even consistency throughout. This treatment, called "wedging," serves the further purpose of removing any extraneous matter that may have been accidentally incorporated in the clay during previous handling. Wedging is an essential step and is fully explained and pictured in later pages.

When properly wedged, clay is ready for shaping. The obliging nature of the material allows it to take practically any shape. As you become sensitive to your material, however, you will find that shapes with soft curves and rounded corners and edges are the most pleasing and practical.

If work is interrupted, or a project too large to complete at one sitting, wrap a damp cloth around it and cover with an upturned bucket or box to keep it from drying out. When resuming work, moisten any stiffened edges before adding fresh clay.

When shaping of the piece is completed, set it aside to dry. Evaporation of the water in the clay will cause it to shrink as it dries. If shrinkage is sudden, or occurs more rapidly in one part of the pot than another, it may warp or crack. Drying should therefore be slow and the piece shielded from drafts and sunlight.

8

A cardboard carton, inverted over the piece, will make a temporary drying box if closed cupboard space isn't available.

When the clay piece has become "leather-hard"—a term used to denote the state in which it is sufficiently stiff to handle without misshaping but not completely dry—spouts, handles and foot rims can be added. Some forms of decoration, such as applying "slip" glazes and the carving or modeling of surfaces, are also done when the piece is leather-hard. After added parts or decorations have also dried in a protected place, the piece can be brought out and allowed to dry completely at room temperature, in sunlight, under an infra-red light or in a slow oven.

Plastic, leather-hard or dry pottery pieces are known as "greenware." A piece in any of these states is delicate and should be lifted and moved with care. Any attempt to grasp or lift it by the rim, handle or spout will likely be disastrous to the piece, although the clay can be reworked. Instead, lift greenware from under or around its base, using both hands.

When greenware is thoroughly air-dried, it is ready for "firing" in a pottery "kiln." Kiln firing could be likened to baking in an oven, except that firing temperatures for pottery clays greatly exceed those possible in a domestic stove. Although it is extremely desirable for the potter to own and operate his own kiln, the beginner can by-pass this part of the work by having greenware fired at a ceramic studio which offers this service. Your ceramic supply dealer can give you information on having work custom-fired in your community.

Some pottery needs to be fired only once to make it fit its purpose. The first firing, known as the "bisque" or "biscuit" firing, is the only one needed for the familiar terra-cotta flower pot, for example. Biscuit ware is usually porous, of the natural color of the clay used, and somewhat rough. Nevertheless, once-fired clay colors and textures are often pleasing for flower pots, fountains, sculptures and other pieces with functions unimpeded by porosity, and these need no further treatment to make them complete.

ERNIE KIM

Lamp base of slab construction
with incised decoration.

Other pottery pieces will be pleasing in use and appearance only if they have been coated with a "glaze." The glaze coating serves to seal and make surfaces smooth and to add color. In most cases glaze coatings are applied to biscuit ware and the piece is then returned to the kiln for the "glost" fire which completes the piece.

Glazes are coatings of glass produced by the fusion of various compounded materials. In the raw state they appear as powders; when mixed with water for use, they become thin creamy pastes in pale tints. The glaze mixture is applied to biscuit ware with a soft brush, by dipping or spraying the piece, or by pouring the glaze over it. Color and surface textures of the glaze develop in the glost firing.

Glazes, in unlimited colors and kinds, are for sale by your ceramic supply dealer. The beginner who is working alone will usually choose from these prepared and ready-to-use glazes and have glazed pieces custom-fired.

From the preceding descriptions, given very briefly here but expanded in detail in later pages, you can see that pottery making has many facets—any one of which may engage your eventual interest beyond all others. Some potters remain forever intrigued by the possibilities of shaping clay. Others find that their interest lies in the firing of it or in the compounding of glazes.

As a novice, you may doubt your ability to cover so many stages. Your doubts should disappear, however, when you realize how many people share your interest in ceramic crafts. Clay is being thumped and wedged, shaped and fired in homes, studios, schools, hospitals and community centers all over this land! If you need it, you'll find ready help in any phase of the work.

By using molds, the pottery-maker can duplicate useful items such as this ash tray which was cast in a two-piece mold.

Coil-built pieces may be utilitarian or decorative, symmetrical or non-symmetrical. Color of owl is terra cotta and white.

LOUISE PFEIFFER

Basic tools include: modeling tools, rulers, sponges, oil cloth, piano wire, dividers, compass, rolling pin, bench whirler.

2 · Tools and Materials

You will need a few inexpensive tools and several essential pieces of equipment before undertaking pottery making. You will also need a supply of clay. The clay, tools and some of the equipment can be purchased from the dealer in ceramic supplies. Locate dealers in your community through the classified section of the telephone book. Quantities of ceramic supplies can be ordered by mail; addresses of these mail order dealers can be noted in advertisements in craft and hobby magazines.

You may already have some of the essentials. The first of these is a substantial work table about 3' x 4' and about 30" high. Work surface can be unpainted wood, linoleum or tempered composition board. It is often convenient to have a separate piece of composition board cut to table top size, thus adapting kitchen table to craft bench at will.

The clay container can be a 10-gallon stoneware crock with a lid or any small tub with cover. It is necessary to have the clay container covered to keep clay plastic and in good working condition. For mixing clay, glazes and plaster you will need one or more enameled or stainless steel bowls or basins. An 8" mixing bowl is suitable.

A piece of 20-gauge piano wire about 3' long —available from your ceramics supplies dealer or at large hardware stores—is needed for cutting clay in wedging.

A "fettling" knife is useful. This has a long, narrow blade specially designed for work with clay. Another clay-working tool is the wooden modeling tool. Buy one about 6" long which has one end flattened and rounded, the other end forming a flat angle.

For making measurements, laying out circles,

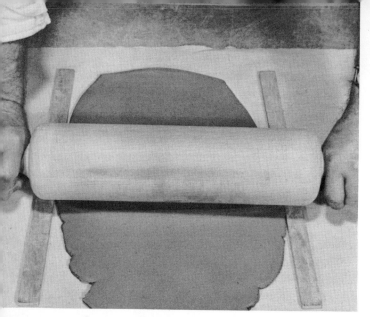

Common rolling pin for making slabs.

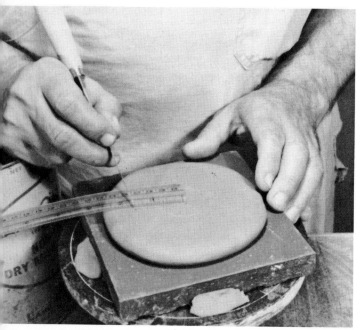

Plastic ruler not affected by moisture.

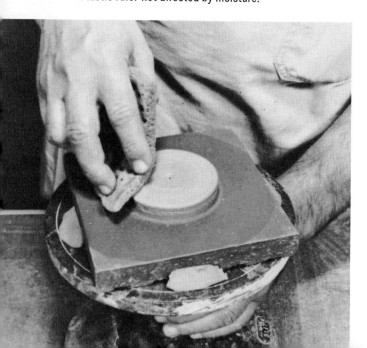

Elephant-ear sponge for finishing.

etc., provide yourself with a 12″ plastic rule— wetting makes wooden ones useless—and a pair of dividers or a compass.

A wooden rolling pin and two pieces of wood ¼″ x 1″ x 18″ are needed for rolling out slabs of clay, the narrow sticks to be used as thickness guides.

Hand-built pieces are easiest to turn and handle generally if they are begun on a porous base, such as an unglazed tile or a plaster bat. Buy several unglazed tiles about 6″ square from the ceramic supply dealer or make a few plaster bats according to directions given in Chapter 3. Plaster bats are very helpful in working with clay. Clay that is too wet to work can be dried quickly by spreading it out on the bat, or wet bats can be placed under clay pieces to keep them damp between working periods.

Although not strictly essential, a bench whirler, or banding wheel, sometimes called a modeling wheel, is very convenient to have. Work placed on a bat on the whirler makes it possible to view all sides of the piece with ease without need for the worker to move around it.

An ice pick or sharp-pointed awl is needed for piercing holes or trimming rims of thrown pieces.

For clean-up work and smoothing clay surfaces, you'll find that nothing works as well as the natural sponge. Have a small "elephant-ear" sponge for smoothing, moistening and rounding edges, and a large wool sponge for lubricating clay and general clean-up.

Cheesecloth, surgical gauze or worn sheeting can be used to wrap clay and unfinished pieces between work periods.

CLAY

The kind of clay you will buy will depend on what you want to make with it and the firing conditions available. This last is a most important consideration in selecting your clay. Do not, for instance, choose a clay which needs a high temperature to bring it to maturity if firing facilities available are limited to those in a lower range. If your first pieces are to be custom-fired, it will be wise to discuss the choice of clay with the kiln operator before making any purchase.

Varieties recommended according to use are pottery and modeling clay, and sculpture clay. These are available in white, buff and reddish terra-cotta color familiar in common bricks and flower pots. The clay particularly desired for larger sculptures contains an added percentage of "grog." Grog is ground-up particles of clay that has been fired. It can be purchased and added to a portion of the pottery clay to adapt it to sculptural uses.

Clay can be purchased in large or small amounts, either in a dry, powdered state or in a moist mass. The price per pound is less when it is purchased in larger quantities. As a starter, buy a 25- or 50-pound package of moist clay body put up in a plastic storage bag. The plastic bag will keep the clay in workable condition for months.

WHAT IS CLAY?

Some craftsmen will be curious concerning the properties and structure of clay at the onset of their interest in ceramics. Others may not ask "What is clay?" until they have handled and worked with it for a time. The following discussion will answer the question in simple terms for those who want to know more about clay than is actually needed merely to make a pot.

When the earth was formed, the dry land was but a rocky crust. Forces such as rain, winds, heat and cold worked on the crust to break it down subsequently into soil. The rocks were of different kinds, and consequently soil formed from them was of different kinds. Sand, for instance, is soil formed from a kind of rock which breaks into millions of smaller rocks. A grain of sand is three-dimensional and may have sharp corners and many facets.

Piano wire separates ware from wheel.

Wooden spatula for welding joints.

Calipers are used for measuring.

A handful of fine, wet sand, squeezed together, will form a mass until the sand dries and water evaporates. A chemist would say that the ions (atoms carrying electric charges) in the water hold the grains together; as soon as electric charges are lost, the sand mass falls apart.

Clay is a different kind of soil. The rock which forms clay is broken down into millions of extremely fine particles which are very thin and flat—like tiny sheets of paper or flat metal plates. Water causes these to stick together. A chemist would say that water increases molecular attraction between clay particles. A simple experiment illustrates this. Wet two flat sheets of glass and lay one atop the other. Lifting the top sheet without also lifting the bottom will be difficult. Try sliding one over the other, and you will find it comparatively easy. Flat, wet clay particles will slide but are held together by the molecular attraction of the water cushion. The result is a soft, pliable mass. This property in clay is known as "plasticity," and it is this that makes clay different from any other soil.

When powdered clay is mixed with water, not all of the tiny particles stack uniformly or fit together perfectly. Minute open spaces are left when particles stand on edge or sideways. These open spaces fill with water to form pores. This condition in clay is called "porosity." The smaller the particles, the more of them there are to fit closely and slide—pores are small and clay is very plastic. It may be necessary to add sand or other coarse material to make clay more porous, so water can evaporate uniformly as it escapes, before this plastic clay can be successfully used by the potter. For instance, a bowl dries and the clay particles which form the walls pull together as the water of the cushion between them evaporates. The walls of the bowl shrink as the clay crystals pull together. The clay becomes harder and stronger as it loses its plasticity, and the strength of the dry clay bowl is the result of the attraction of the flat clay crystal surfaces. If clay is too coarse-grained or contains an excessive amount of sand or other coarse material, the bowl will lack strength.

Should you put water in a dry clay bowl, it would disintegrate to become once again a soft mass of plastic clay. Before the form can become permanent it must be fired in a pottery kiln. Changes in the structure of the clay take place when it is fired. Particles pull together still more tightly than they did while simply drying. This is because drying dispelled the "water of plasticity." There is a second type of water in clay not evaporated by mere air-drying. This is the "chemically combined water" which is a part of the clay particle, and it is the driving off of this water by heat that causes the clay to shrink still further in firing.

Clay in its pure state requires very high temperatures to become sufficiently rock-like to be durable—such high temperatures, in fact, that it is impractical to use pure clay alone to make ware.

Most clays contain many impurities. If clay has moved from the location in which it was formed, it has picked up many more impurities in its travels which have become ground in with the clay particles. These impurities are usually of such a nature that they melt into glass when clay is fired. The glass film binds pure clay together. The melting of these impurities to make glass is the process known to the potter as "vitrification." Amount of vitrification depends on amounts of glass-forming materials present and the temperature to which wares are fired.

Some clays are formed by rocks which have been covered over with marshes and swamps. Decaying weeds and grasses formed carbonic acid and marsh gases. Acid, gases and swamp water broke down the rock and dissolved the soluble materials in it, leaving a bed of comparatively pure clay. This clay is known as

14

"primary" or "residual." Residual clays are usually refractory, which means that they withstand a very high degree of heat without melting. These clays usually fire white or pale cream color, are not very plastic, and must be blended with other clays and minerals for making ware. These are the clays used to make porcelain.

As other clays were formed by the breaking up of rocks, they were picked up and carried by streams and rivers—sometimes for great distances. As they traveled, particles were ground finer and finer and they joined company with fragments of other rocks, such as limestone and shale and particles of metal and vegetable matter. When the stream carrying the combined particles reached a lake or settling area, a bed of "secondary," or "sedimentary," clay was formed. Some sedimentary clay may be spoken of as "earthenware" clay. The group of earthenware clays includes most of the shales and surface clays prevalent in the eastern part of the United States. These clays fire red or brown because of the high iron content. These red-burning clays are very fusible—when heated to vitrification point they fuse, melt, and the ware loses shape because of the large percentage of impurities.

Sedimentary clays vary in that some did not travel so far or met different company on the way. One of these, containing a medium percentage of glass-forming impurities, is known as "stoneware" clay. Stoneware clays are usually tan, buff, gray or brown when fired. They are used for cooking wares and decorative pottery.

SYNTHETIC OR COMPOUNDED CLAYS

Many clay bodies are compounded in the laboratory through experimental blends of various materials. Bodies are compounded to suit them to the making of different types of ware —to make them more or less plastic, to make them vitrify at certain temperatures and to control porosity. As a potter you will be offered

Stoneware is fine-textured but sturdy, vitrifies at high temperatures.

Earthenware is coarse-grained, thick-walled, easiest for beginning potter.

15

a compounded clay body suitable to your uses.

When you shop for clay, you may hear the many varieties called by names which are sometimes confusing to the uninitiated. The most common classifications are earthenware, stoneware and porcelain clays. Classification is based on the nature of the clay and not on the finished appearance of the products made from each type of clay. The following paragraphs describe the characteristics of these clays separately.

EARTHENWARE

Natural clay bodies coming under this heading are red or brown when fired to maturity. Maturing range is usually between 1800 and 2100 degrees Fahrenheit. Compounded earthenware bodies may be any color, red, brown, tan, buff, white or cream, and may require temperatures as high as 2300 degrees F. for maturing.

Some characteristics of earthenware are: comparatively coarse grain structure, low chipping resistance in finished ware, and deformation of the ware if fired to point of vitrification of the clay body. When a fragment of earthenware which has been fired to maturity is examined under the microscope, it is seen that the grains in the body structure have retained individuality. Only partial vitrification has taken place, and single clay particles can be pushed from the mass with a hard steel point.

To be appropriate to the material, earthenware products will be rather thick-walled, simply formed for straightforward, unsophisticated effects. Beginners will do well to choose an earthenware body in order to take advantage of affinity of material for the kind of ware best undertaken while skills are developing.

STONEWARE

This may be either a natural or compounded body. It will be more refined than earthenware, is usually buff, tan or gray when fired, and in most instances matures satisfactorily at temperatures from 2100 to 2300 degrees F. Grain structure is finer than that of earthenware clay; products made of it have greater resistance to chipping and the strength of the material makes it suitable for kitchen and baking ware. Microscopic examination of a broken fragment of fired ware will show loss of identity of grains, a greater degree of vitrification than seen in the earthenware shard, and it will not be possible to separate any single grain from the mass with a steel point.

Products appropriate to this material will have walls of medium thickness and more refined in form than those made of earthenware.

PORCELAIN

This is the aristocrat of clay bodies—the most highly refined of all clay body types. It is rarely found as a natural body but is compounded as a blend of kaolins, china clays, ball clays and feldspars. Characteristic properties are: extreme fineness of grain structure, hardness and toughness when fired, resistance to acids, translucence, and complete vitrification when fired to maturity. Color is usually white or blue-white when fired, and maturing temperatures are between 2250 and 2500 degrees F., depending on body composition. Examination of a broken fired fragment shows the whole mass as vitrified to resemble glass in that no particles can be seen separately or removed and the material will not scratch under a steel point.

Porcelain products will be thin-walled, delicate and refined in line and sophisticated in shape.

Products made of any of the types of clay described will vary in quality according to the potter's skill, ability and understanding of his materials. Complete understanding of the possibilities and potentialities of any clay body will come only through actual working experience with it.

The above bodies are available from supply houses. You can prepare the following.

LOW-FIRE PORCELAIN

Bodies which become vitreous at low temperatures may be called low-fire porcelain, synthetic porcelain, or soft-paste porcelain. Owing to their high content of flux (glassforming material), they become very soft at maturing temperature and when being fired should be supported evenly on a tile coated with kiln wash rather than on stilts or pins. Since they may contain less clay than other bodies, bentonite is sometimes used to increase plasticity. They should be used to make small pieces and ornaments, since large pieces may slump when fired.

Cone 07–05 Body

English china clay*	20 pbw
Kentucky special ball clay	23
Cullet (powdered glass)	22
Kona A3 feldspar	35
Bentonite	3

*Moore & Munger, 33 Rector Street, New York City.

Screen dry, add 60% water, grind 3 to 4 hours on ball mill.

Nephelene Syenite Body, Which Becomes Vitreous and Translucent at Cone 3

Nephelen syenite	55 pbw
Kentucky ball clay	10
Edgar plastic kaolin	25
Flint	10

Bentonite, 2% to 3% addition
To avoid lumps, screen bentonite with other materials before adding water.

SELF-GLAZING BODY (Egyptian Paste)

A self-glazing body contains some soluble substance which crystallizes on the surface of the piece as it dries and melts into a glaze when fired. The body must contain enough frit or cullet to act as a flux and tighten the pores of the clay. It must have enough soluble

Japanese Raku ware tea bowl made in 1790 is typical of present-day Raku bowls.

crystalline material to settle on the surface and form a coating of glaze. It must contain enough clay to permit forming. In addition, it should contain enough flint to prevent crazing. Such a body is called Egyptian paste from its use by ancient Egyptian potters. The glaze crystallizes on the surface of the ware as it dries, so do not scrape the piece, and trim only enough to form the foot.

Mix coloring oxide with the body before adding water. Since the paste may be difficult to manipulate on the wheel, only small forms should be attempted.

A body developed by Cecile McCann, which can be thrown, will have turquoise glaze when 2% copper carbonate is added, purple glaze when 1% manganese carbonate is added, and a strong yellow-green glaze when 1% lead chromate is added.

17

Self-Glazing Body (cone 06)

Powdered flint	35 pbw
Cullet	20
Kentucky ball clay #4	23
Crystalline soda or soda ash	4
Bentonite	3

Egyptian Paste (cone 07)

Ivory Fat ball clay	27 pbw
Nephelene Syenite	20
Flint	35
SS-65 powdered (Cal Quartz) †	5
Soda ash	7
Copper carbonate	3

†Philadelphia Quartz Co. of Berkeley, California.

Another self-glazing body, which fires turquoise mottled with black areas and has a surface texture similar to that of Egyptian scarabs, and which can also be thrown for small forms, was developed by Arthur Baggs.

Prepare self-glazing bodies by screening all materials together, then add water until mixture is consistency of cream and hand-grind thoroughly in mortar. Permit body to air-dry until it can be hand-wedged and thrown. When leather hard, trim foot, dry, and fire setting level and flat in kiln on slab of porous fire brick coated with kiln wash.

Raku bowl, pinch-formed. Outside bottom half is black, inside and top half is brown.

RAKU WARE

Japanese Raku ware has been made for centuries and is a special favorite with tea ceremony devotees. The body for Raku ware is a high-fire plastic fire clay mixed with fine grog or sand. Traditionally, Raku ware is made **tebineri** (without the use of the wheel). Forms such as tea bowls should be pinch-formed or coil-built with walls 1/2″ to 3/8″ thick. After forming, the ware is biscuited at a low temperature (about 1800 degrees F.), a lead glaze is brushed on, and the ware is fired again until the glaze is melted. As soon as the glaze is melted, the ware is removed from the kiln with tongs. The soft underfired body and removal from the kiln while red-hot assures a crazed glaze. The Japanese say such a combination will not cause a harsh discordant sound when the tea is whisked.

A Raku Body (biscuit fire at cone 07)

Lincoln fire clay	70 pbw
Fine grog	30

The body of the Raku bowl shown is sculpture clay mixed with sand. The piece was pinch-formed and biscuited, the outside bottom half was coated with black glaze, and the inside and top half of the outside was coated with brown glaze. As soon as the glaze melted, the piece was removed from the kiln with tongs, cooled in sawdust, then dipped in a bucket of water.

Black Raku Glaze

Frit #3110	20 pbw
White lead	60
Flint	20
Black stain	2
Cobalt carbonate	1
GMC gum powder	1

Brown Raku Glaze

Frit #3396	60
Cullet	20
White lead	20
GMC gum powder	1

BEATRICE WAX

Properly wedged,
the clay ball is smooth
and free of air pockets.

3 · Preliminary Steps

The basic steps to be followed in the handling of clay are the same regardless of kind of clay used or the purpose for which it is intended. Some of these, suggested in previous pages, are amplified here to describe procedures in detail.

MIXING POWDERED CLAY

Clay purchased in powder form is mixed with water to make it a plastic mass. To mix, fill large dishpan or small tub about one-third full of water. Sift clay over water, one handful at a time, until clay settles on top of the water to make a coating about 1″ thick. Cover pan with paper or cloth and let the unstirred mixture set overnight. On the following day mix and stir it thoroughly. If mass is too thick to knead, add more water. If too thin, add dry clay. Clay is in a state to store when it is soft and pliable but does not stick to the hands. Since clay improves with aging in a damp condition, mix as far ahead of time of use as you can. Wrap clay in damp cloth and store in covered crock for at least one week before using.

RECONDITIONING CLAY

Scraps of dry clay and broken ware that was not fired can be reclaimed and reused. Spread lumps and scraps out on a hard surface and pound them with a mallet or piece of wood used paddle-fashion until largest remaining pieces are about the size of a walnut. Put reclaimed clay into a large pan and cover with water, allowing an excess of about 1″ above top of clay. Permit clay to soak without stir-

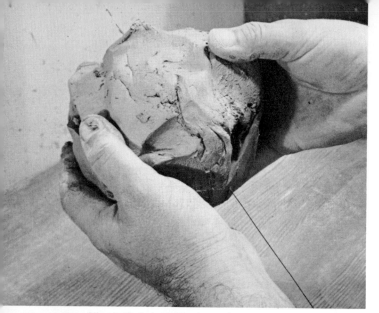

Slice ball of clay with piano wire.

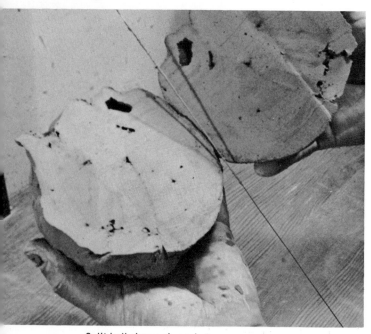

Split ball shows air pockets.

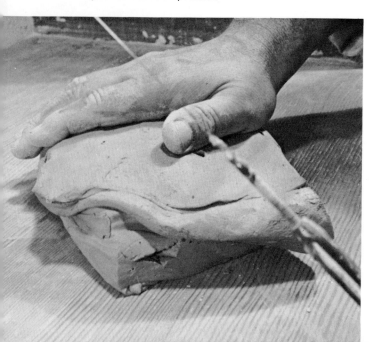

Clay is slammed on table to drive
air out of ball, make it pliable.

ring for at least twelve hours. If, by that time, the clay has soaked up all the water, cover with water once more and let it set an additional six hours. Then stir thoroughly, breaking any remaining lumps with your hands, and add dry powdered clay slowly until it can be kneaded into a mass of the proper consistency.

If you have no powdered clay, ladle the reclaimed clay onto a large, dry plaster bat. Turn it over as soon as it can be handled, watching to see that clay does not get too dry. When putty-like, knead it thoroughly and store. Any clay too wet to work can be conditioned by kneading it on a dry plaster bat.

If clay becomes overly stiff in crock, despite damp cloths, it can usually be reconditioned by punching holes in it and filling the holes with water, then covering the whole with a saturated cloth. Let clay set for a day or so and then take from the crock and rework.

Clay will not deteriorate or suffer from inattention even if left in the crock for long periods. It may mold, but this will not hurt it. To be kept workable over long periods, however, it should have extra cloth wrappings—turkish toweling is excellent—and wrappings should be sprinkled with water occasionally.

WEDGING

When a portion of the clay is taken from the crock to be shaped, it must first be wedged. This is the process which is employed to force any air bubbles from the mass and to make it uniform in texture throughout. Bubbles, or "blebs" as they are sometimes called, will not cause clay products to explode in the kiln as is popularly believed, but they will cause the piece to crack during either drying or firing. A bubble in the wall of a piece being thrown is particularly annoying.

To wedge your clay, first roll and pat it into a flat rectangular mass. Cut this in two by slicing it with the length of piano wire held taut in the hands, or by bringing it down over a wire stretched between an upright fastened to one edge of the table and the opposite table edge. Slap the two pieces together smartly on the table top with cut edges out. Reshape rectangle, cut in two with wire and again slam pieces on table, one on top of the other with cut ends out. Repeat until wire-cut surfaces show the inside of the mass to be free from holes and of a smooth and even texture throughout.

Wedging clay is sometimes likened to kneading bread dough. In reality they are opposing processes in that wedging is done to eliminate air from the mass and the kneading of dough is done to incorporate air into it. Slap and smack the clay mass with palms of the hands —rather than folding and punching it with knuckles or tips of fingers and thereby making air-catching holes in it.

When a project is complete, rewedge remaining clay, shape it into a ball, and wrap it for storage in the crock. Clay used for practice throwing on the wheel is also rewedged before returning it to storage. As the clay used in this manner will likely be too wet for immediate wedging, place it on a plaster bat until dry enough to handle.

MAKING PLASTER BATS

As the plaster-topped wedging table and bats of various shapes and sizes are indispensable to the potter working with clay in any considerable amounts, directions for mixing plaster and pouring bats are given here.

To make a plaster bat you will need potter's plaster purchased from your ceramic supply house, water, a mixing pan, and a form of the size and shape desired for the bat. A cardboard box will make a form for the square or rectangular bat; a cake or pie tin for the round one. The form needn't be strong or durable, but it must be leakproof or plaster will flow out while still liquid. Seal any cracks or broken corners in paper box forms with clay coils smoothed over them on the inside of the box.

The box can be torn away after the plaster has hardened. Paper pie plates can be used in the same way.

If metal pie plates are to be used, oil them lightly before filling with plaster. To simplify removing the bat from a straight-sided metal cake pan, line the sides with a coating of clay $\frac{1}{2}''$ thick. When plaster is set, the clay liner can be dug out with the wooden modeling tool and bat dislodged easily by tapping the bottom of the pan.

Pie-size bats should be at least 1″ thick, for plaster is brittle and thin sections are easily broken. Larger bats are best made 2″ or 3″ thick, and the wedging table top may be 5″ or 6″ thick.

SOME APPROXIMATE PROPORTIONS FOR BATS

To make bat approximately:

4″ x 4″—add 11 oz. plaster to $\frac{1}{2}$ pint water

6″ x 6″—add 1 lb. 6 oz. plaster to 1 pint water

5″ x 10″—add 2 lbs. 12 oz. plaster to 1 quart water

9″ x 10″—add 4 lbs. 2 oz. plaster to 3 pints water

10″ x 10″—add 5 lbs. 8 oz. plaster to 2 quarts water

To mix plaster in larger amounts, use approximately:

$2\frac{1}{2}$ quarts of water with 6 lbs. 14 oz. plaster

3 quarts water with 8 lbs. 4 oz. plaster

4 quarts water with 11 lbs. plaster

5 quarts water with 13 lbs. 8 oz. plaster

6 quarts water with 16 lbs. 8 oz. plaster

To estimate amounts of liquid plaster needed to fill a form, first judge volume of water required to fill it and allow a little over. The entire form should be filled with one batch of plaster as layers of plaster do not always join well and a bat made in two pours may split.

PLASTER BAT. 1. Sift plaster onto water by handfuls.

To mix the plaster, first put the required amount of water in the mixing bowl. Sift the dry plaster powder through the fingers, one handful at a time, onto the water at the center of the bowl. Continue to add plaster without stirring or shaking the mixture until it stands in a cone $1\frac{1}{2}''$ to $2''$ above the water at bowl center. Wait until the cone has absorbed enough water to wet it through—usually takes one or two minutes—then immerse hand in mixture and stir gently around and around until plaster mix coats the hand like a glove. Avoid splashy vigorous movements while stirring plaster as these result in the incorporation of unwanted air in the mix.

When mixture forms a creamy coating over the hand it is ready to pour. Have form on a level surface and fill it smoothly and quickly, again without splashing. Plaster sets quickly. It goes through a heating process as it hardens, and as soon as it has heated and cooled it will be stiff enough to remove from the form. However, it is best to wait about thirty minutes after pouring before removal. Scrape edges of the fresh bat with a knife to remove any sharp fins or chips and give them a final smoothing with a damp paper towel before setting the bat away to dry completely.

An immediate clean-up after plaster pouring is important. Wipe plaster from mixing bowl with disposable paper towels or crumpled newspaper. Wash any remaining plaster from the bowl and pour this water, and that used to rinse your hands as well, outside. Never pour plaster rinsings in plumbing drains as it will clog them.

2. Pour plaster into form smoothly and quickly.

3. Scrape sharp fins and chips from edges of bat.

Hippopotamus made by pinch-modeled technique shows delightful possibilities of this method.

4 · The Pinch Method

When you pinch a pottery form from a ball of plastic clay, you are following a method practiced by potters for thousands of years. Oriental craftsmen, in particular, have found it a way to produce beautiful forms, and some of the most highly prized bowls used in the Japanese tea ceremonies were made by pinching.

Making a pinched pot is an excellent manner in which to make the acquaintance of the properties of clay. Pots made in this way should be small but they can nevertheless fill many uses. Pinch pots serve as individual nut or candy bowls, relish dishes, ash trays, match holders, and as the small dish used on the stove for receiving the stirring spoon called a "spoon drip."

Clay used to make the pinched form should be fine-grained and plastic, free from grog or coarse sand particles.

"HANDY" ASH TRAY

A convenient ash tray which fits the hand is made as follows: Cut a piece about the size of a golf ball from a wedged mass and roll and pat it round. Support clay ball on the palm of your left hand and apply downward pressure in the exact top center of the ball with the thumb of your right hand. Bring fingers of the right hand against the outside surface of the ball in a pinching motion. While pinching the clay with the right hand, lift and shift it slightly, turning the ball one finger-width in a counterclockwise direction. Bring the right

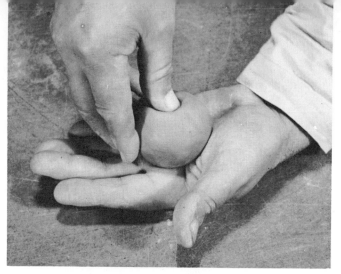

1. Press thumb into clay ball held in left hand.

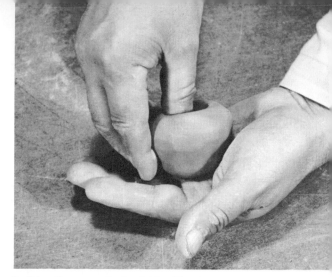

2. Bring fingers against outside of bowl.

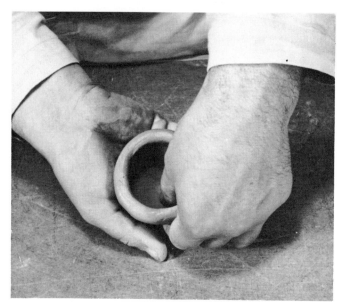

3. Pinch with right hand, turn with left.

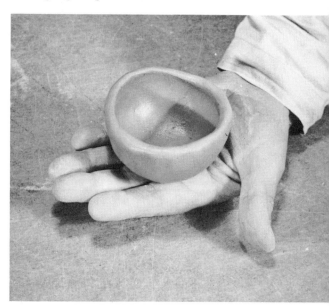

4. Thin out walls to uniform ¼″ thickness.

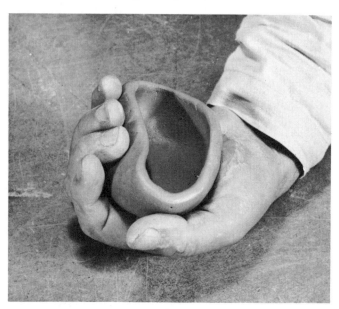

5. Slowly close hand to squeeze to shape.

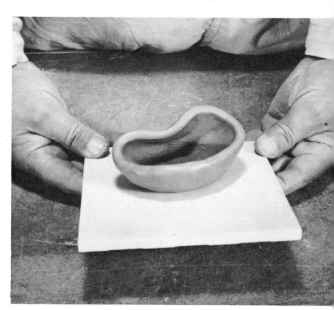

6. Set on flat surface to flatten bottom.

hand back the width of one finger and repeat the step. You will find as you work that the thumb gradually sinks into the clay ball and that the wall between the thumb and fingers thins and expands.

As the form expands, pinch the bottom of the piece between the end of the thumb and middle finger of the right hand until the bottom is about ¼″ thick. If edges show signs of cracking, moisten lightly with a sponge and gently rub the rim to close cracks. Thin out the walls by pinching until they are of a uniform thickness of about ¼″.

To give the ash tray its free form, hold the bowl loosely in the left hand. Slowly close the hand to gently squeeze to shape as desired. Set the tray on a flat surface to flatten bottom, and the piece may then be set away to dry for future firing.

THE PINCHED BOWL

Though the procedure for making the pinched bowl is related to that for the handy ash tray, they are not identical. For this project more clay is used and you will work with both hands, while the clay rests on a paper which permits it to move freely on the table top.

Pinched bowl formed from orange-sized ball of clay has glazed foot-ring.

The pinched bowl shown above is useful as a cereal, grapefruit, nut or candy bowl. To make it, you will need about 1½ pounds of clay. If you have no scales or means of weighing the clay, a piece about the size of a regulation baseball is the proper size. You should have a piece of folded newspaper or paper towel to permit the clay to move freely on the table top.

Pat the clay into a ball, place the ball of clay on the paper. Place the ends of both thumbs

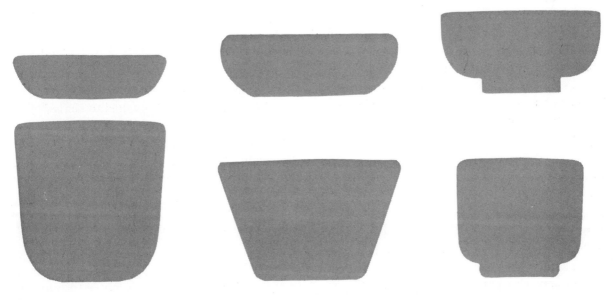

Suggested shapes for pinch pots.

25

Asymmetrical dishes are easily pinched from hand-sized slab of clay.

on top of the clay ball in the exact center or as near so as possible. Press downward lightly with the thumbs and exert a mild pinching pressure between the thumbs and fingers of both hands. As you pinch the clay, turn it one finger-width in a clockwise motion. Repeat the operation until there is ½″ of clay between the ends of your thumbs and the paper. The ball of clay will have expanded until you have a hole about 2″ in diameter in the center of the clay ball. Continue pinching and spreading the ball until you have a bowl of the size and shape you wish.

THE ALL-PURPOSE DISH

The asymmetrical pottery forms shown above are all-purpose dishes particularly useful on the dinner or luncheon table. They can be made with any desired variation in form. They can be made in any size you wish, though when flat forms such as this are too large, they often warp (twist) during drying or firing.

To make a piece like those above, you will need a piece of medium plastic clay about the size of a large cucumber. Pat the coil between the hands, then pinch it until it is uniformly about ⅜″ in thickness. The resulting pancake will be somewhat larger than your right hand, and a somewhat irregular rectangle in shape. Support the clay pancake on the palm of your

left hand or place it on a paper on the table top, and gently pinch the edge between the thumb and the fingers of your right hand with the thumb on the upper and the fingers against the lower side of the pancake. As you pinch the clay, gently turn the edge upward. Work all of the way around the pancake, using the same amount of pressure each time you pinch the edge. Uniformity of pressure assures you of uniform wall thickness. Avoid sharp angles or corners either on the inside or outside for greater ease in glazing and later in washing after use.

THE PINCH-MODELED FIGURE

Making a small pinch-modeled figure offers an excellent opportunity for the development of the creative imagination in both children and adults. Children not only enjoy this method of making small figures—they often show more ability at the start than adults.

Figures made in this way should be small. Start with a portion of wedged clay of medium-soft consistency about the size and shape of a cheese-spread glass. Grasp this elongated cylinder in the right hand and squeeze. While still holding the clay, strike one end of the wad lightly on the table top to flatten it.

Set flattened end of wad on a tile, plaster bat or bench whirler so work can be readily turned and seen from all sides during the modeling.

Examine the squeezed clay for suggestions of form or figure and add any details needed to amplify it. Ears can be pinched to shape, eyes developed by pinching bits from the mass, and parts of the shape accented with finger modeling. Delicacy of detail is neither desirable nor necessary in this type of figure, and its charm will be in its simplicity. Let the fingers be the only modeling tools, and remove none of the clay of the original cylinder for the most direct effects.

When modeling of the figure is complete, let it dry very slowly and completely before firing.

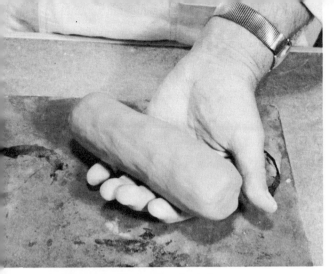

1. Start with cylinder of wedged clay.

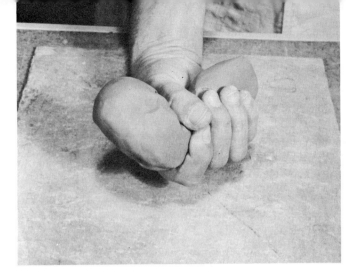

2. Squeeze clay cylinder.

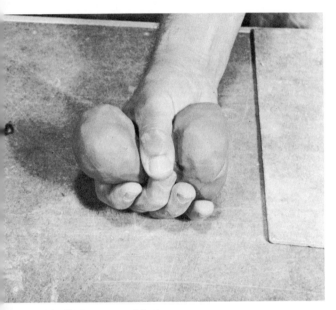

3. Flatten one end for base.

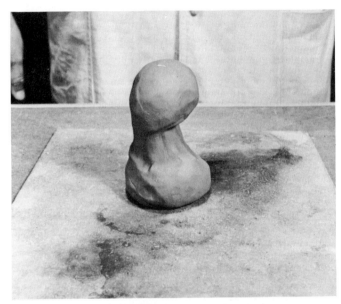

4. Set clay on end, view from all sides.

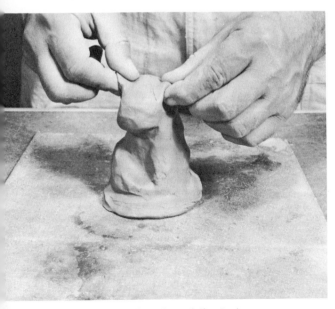

5. Let fingers be the only modeling tools.

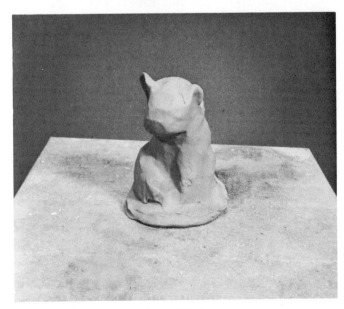

6. Finished form is simple, free of detail.

THE COMBINED PINCHED FORM

Practice making various-sized pinch bowls. You'll find that with practice each one will be better than the last. When you have mastered uniform wall thickness and control of form you are ready to combine two pinch bowls to make a closed form, such as two half-spheres to make a hollow sphere, or two half egg shapes to make an ovoid. Or make a bottle, as shown by James Lovera in the accompanying photographic series.

Start with two well-wedged balls of clay the same size. Pinch each ball into a good-sized bowl shaped like half an egg. Check diameter and wall thickness of both bowls with calipers and ruler to be sure they are constant and the same. The inside of a bottle is hard to clean, so smooth the inside surface of both bowls by pressing with a large smooth pebble. To insure a solid joint later, smooth and carefully level the rims. Place the bowls rim down on a smooth level surface and set them aside to become leather hard. When they are hard enough to handle without losing their shape, score the rims of both bowls with the tip of your fettling knife. Coat the scored surfaces with slip, and press the bowls solidly together, being careful not to distort them. Use the tip of your modeling tool to press the clay firmly toward the joint on both sides of it, while at the same time deeply scoring the surface. Now roll out a coil ½" in diameter. Coat the scored surface of the sphere with slip, place the coil in position on the joint, and press it firmly into place. Weld the coil in both directions from the joint, then paddle the coil to contour of form. Paddle one end of the form to make a flattened base. Cut hole in other end, and score surface around hole.

Pinch a neck from a small ball of clay and flare one end of it for a lip. Score the unflared end, add slip to the scored surfaces of neck and bowl, and attach. When the piece is leather hard, carve decoration.

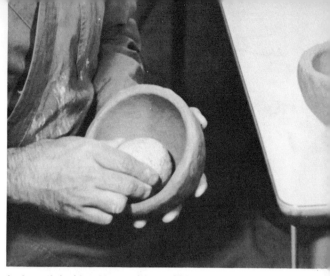

1. Smooth inside of bowl with a pebble.

4. Add slip and place coil on top of joint.

7. Paddle coil to contour of form.

2. Measure wall thickness with a ruler.

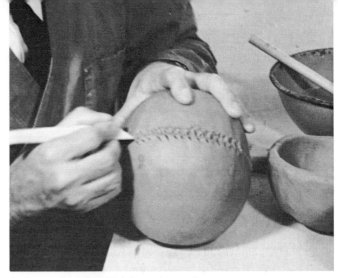

3. Press clay toward joint, scoring surface.

5. Press coil firmly into place.

6. Weld coil in both directions from joint.

8. Paddle one end of form for base.

9. Attach neck with slip and weld.

Good coil-built pottery can often match grace of wheel-formed products.

RUTH SPOON

5 · Building with Coils

Building forms with clay coils is one of the easiest and most rewarding ways of making pottery. Use of this method permits the beginner to make pieces in any desired shape and size and allows the experienced craftsman to develop forms not readily achieved by other means.

Almost any clay can be used for coil building. It should be plastic, but moderately stiff, to allow the coils to be lifted without undue stretching or loss of shape.

Possibilities of form in coil-built ware are unlimited. Make your coiled pieces round, oval, rectangular or in irregular shapes. Your products can be bowls, vases, jugs, pitchers, can-

nisters or lamp bases—to name but a few of the possibilities. Many of these will be built as coiled cylinders—others as expanding coiled forms. Procedures in making both follow.

THE COILED CYLINDER

Take a small portion of the three or four pounds of wedged clay to be used for the cylindrical form and pat it into a ball. Place ball on an unglazed tile or partially saturated plaster bat, using a bench whirler if one is available. Pat ball to make a pancake of uniform thickness. Thickness of base will vary according to planned finished dimensions of the piece. A pot 3″ in diameter will ordinarily have a base about $\frac{3}{8}$″ thick; one 6″ will have a base about

Coil-built forms can be symmetrical or asymmetrical. Pitcher has coil spout and handle.

LOUISE PFEIFFER

½″ thick; the pot 9″ in diameter will have a base about ¾″ thick, etc.

Use compass or dividers to outline the circular base. Cut through the clay along outline, holding knife vertically, and remove excess clay.

To make the coils which will form the wall of the pot, first make cigar-shaped wads of clay. Roll these under the fingers on a damp, but not wet, table top. Spread the fingers on both hands, resting them lightly on the clay. As you roll it forward under your spread fingers, also move hands outward to lengthen coil. Roll the coil forward for a distance of about 12″, then roll it back again. Repeat until coil is made. If clay is stiff or cracks, the table top may be

Coil construction may be left exposed, as with this bottle; or smoothed over, as with the vase.

RUTHADELL HORAN

too dry. If it sticks, table top is too wet or clay too soft. Hard pressing on the coil will flatten it or make sections of varying diameters. Try to make it a smooth, even rod.

Coils should be about as big around as a lead pencil for the piece 3″ in diameter. Larger pieces will use larger coils: the 6″ cylinder calls for coils ⅜″, the 9″ diameter ½″ coils, etc.

Place the first coil on the top edge of the base so it is completely around, and directly above, the edge. Cut off excess. Press ends of coil firmly together and weld the joint by dragging a bit of the clay from one end of the coil across the other. Weld joint all around. Use the first finger of the right hand to press the first coil firmly against the base as you support it with the fingers of the left. Weld coil to base on both inside and out by dragging small amounts of clay from the coil across the joint to seal it completely.

Place each additional coil squarely on top of that below, welding ends and joints between coils on both inside and outside of piece as you build. Be sure to have the ends of the coil come at different locations in the wall each time.

If coils are added too rapidly, wall of the piece will sag. To prevent this, allow coils to stiffen slightly before adding new ones. A strong union between coils is essential, however, so moist clay must not be added to any that has become rigid. If top coil becomes stiff, chop light serrations in it with knife and wrap with a wet cloth and allow to stand until the clay rim has regained plasticity. Then continue to add coils until piece is of desired height.

THE COILED EXPANDING FORM

Prepare base and make coils as for the straight-sided cylinder. To make form expand outward, make coil slightly longer and place each coil toward the outer edge of the preceding one. To draw form in, place added coils toward inner edges of preceding ones. Weld ends and joints as previously described.

1. Measure diameter of base with rule.

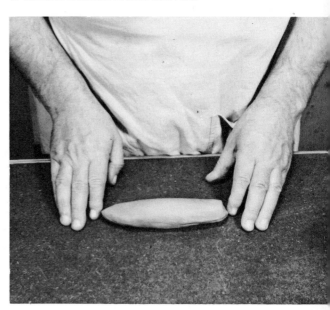

4. Make cigar-shaped wad of clay for coil.

7. Place first coil around top of base.

2. Cut by turning base, holding knife.

3. Remove excess clay, return it to crock.

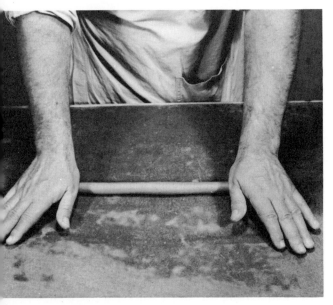

5. Roll back and forth, stretching coil.

6. Try to make smooth, even rod of clay.

8. Weld first coil to base, inside and out.

9. Place subsequent coils directly on top.

Expanding form made by adding larger coils.

To draw in, place coils on inner edge.

When wall weight extends beyond the base, the form tends to sag unless lower coils are allowed to stiffen slightly. Work on several pieces at once or allow the single project to set in warm air for a short period until it stiffens slightly before adding coils.

USING TEMPLATES

To control the shape of a coil-built form, you will need to use a cardboard guide known as a "template." This guide, which you can easily make yourself, is helpful in forming large pieces, such as a vase or a bottle; and its use is mandatory in making matching pieces, such as a pair of lamp bases or a set of mugs.

To make a template, first select the desired shape. Then, using paper ruled off in squares (available from stationery stores), draw the outline of the shape. To enlarge the shape, once it's drawn, count squares covered by any part of it, and draw an equal number of larger squares on paper. Draw the profile outline in the large squares exactly as you see it in the small ones, using same number of squares.

A template assures symmetry. Coil-built asymmetrical forms are made without the use of a template, so careful planning before building is necessary. Some preliminary sketches of the form to be made may help in the planning. Construction of an asymmetrical form is the same as for other coil-

built forms. It is also possible to start out building a symmetrical form and then alter its symmetry in various ways before it has become leather hard: by pressing the wall with the hand from the inside or from the outside. Or, both inside and outside pressures may be used. The symmetry of a form may also be changed by paddling the surface in various ways. A template can be made as follows:

Cut out the form, fold it down the center, and transfer the half-pattern to a cardboard rectangle large enough to accommodate it. Locate the bottom of the half-shape in the lower left-hand corner of the cardboard. Bottom edge of cardboard rectangle should be square with the profile center line. Cut along profile line with a sharp knife or a single-edged razor blade. The cardboard with proposed pot shape cut away is your template.

Use the template by placing it beside the coiled shape as coils are added. Check around the piece frequently to be sure you are not stretching coils. Do not use template as a scraper.

SURFACE TEXTURES

In forming the coiled pot you will find that you can smooth one coil into the next to make a surface of a uniform pebbled texture, or allow each to remain rounded, producing a ribbed, corrugated effect. The smoothed coils can be smoothed still further by rubbing them with a shiny, hard pebble or the bowl of a kitchen spoon. Do not use sandpaper or steel wool, as these will affect the glaze. Combine the corrugated, finger-smoothed or polished surfaces for interesting variations in texture in your coiled pieces.

LARGE COIL-BUILT FORMS

Once the fundamentals of coil building have been mastered, you are ready to build some large forms for use in the garden, on the patio, or by the fireplace. An unusual method for making large coil-built forms is the paddle and anvil technique used by the southeastern American Indians hundreds of years ago. To use this process you will need a good-sized anvil over which to form the ware. The Indians used a boulder shaped somewhat like a large ice cream cone resting on its rim, and having a broad and somewhat flattened or rounded point.

If you cannot find such a boulder that is the right size and shape to use for an anvil, cast a large, solid block of plaster, then carve, scrape, file, and sand it until you have an appropriate cone-shaped hump. A conical anvil shape without any undercuts is necessary in order that the completed clay form can move upward on the anvil as it shrinks while drying, without cracking or splitting.

The shaping paddle should be of sturdy ¾″ wood, about 6″ to 8″ long, and 4″ wide, and about a third of its length should be shaped into a handle. All edges of the paddle should be well-rounded to avoid sharp wedge cuts in the clay. A butter paddle may be used, although it is somewhat light in weight.

Roll out a number of coils at least 1″ in diameter, then keep the coils covered with a damp cloth while working. Drape a piece of burlap smoothly over the anvil, place a thick pancake of clay on top, and paddle it flat. This will be the bottom of the finished piece. Now lap the first coil about a third of its thickness over the edge of the base and weld it firmly on the outside of the base. Repeat this procedure with successive coils.

Combined pinched forms may be paddled into non-symmetrical forms or may have added spouts or necks of slabs or coils.

Coil and slab forms may have decorative treatment as a part of building process or they may be decorated when leather hard.

35

1. Build ⅓ of the form, then shape.

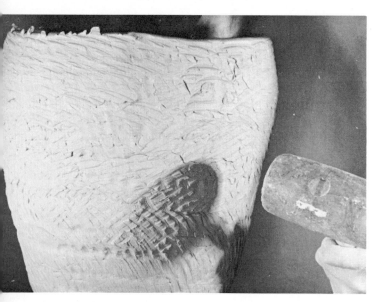

2. Be sure to cover all of the surface.

3. Add the neck and finish by hand.

Make sure all of the coils are pressed solidly together before welding. When you have the coiled piece built to about two-thirds of its final size, start at the base and paddle all around the form, working from the base to the rim. Use the same pressure each time you strike the clay with the paddle to insure uniform wall thickness. The clay will stretch as it is paddled, and the finished form will be a fourth to a third taller than when paddling was started. When the clay is hard enough to handle, remove the form from the anvil, carefully remove the burlap from the clay (watch out for spots that may stick), finish the foot rim, dry, and fire. If the paddle sticks to clay surface, the paddle may be carved, wrapped with cord, or covered with cloth. This will prevent sticking and it will also provide a nicely textured surface.

THE STRIKING PROCESS

The Korean and Japanese version of the paddle and anvil technique is called the striking process. In the accompanying photographs, Joe Hysong demonstrates the use of this process to make a large vase form.

For the striking process, the anvil—made of wood, biscuited clay, or plaster—should be smaller than that used previously. It should be the right size to hold comfortably in your hand. It should be shaped like a well-rounded stuffed pillow and should have no sharp edges. The striking implement may be either a wooden mallet with grooves carved into the face to keep it from sticking to the clay, or a paddle, as described above.

Roughly coil-build about a third of the form, then shape it by supporting the clay on the inside with the anvil as you strike the outside surface with the mallet or paddle. Be sure to move the anvil so it is directly opposite the mallet each time the clay is struck. Also, be sure to cover all the surface of the form.

Indian burial urn with paddled design, made by paddle and anvil technique. Height 17″.

Combined pinched forms: Small-neck bottle, paddled vase, bottle with coil neck.

After shaping, set the form aside for three or four hours to harden. Keep the top coil covered with a damp cloth. As soon as the form will support the weight, build the second third and shape it in the same manner as you did the first third. Be sure to work over carefully the area where the two sections join. After another hardening interval, add the final third and shape it as before. As soon as the form has hardened enough to support the neck, build the neck, attach it, and finish it by hand.

The foot of large forms need not be trimmed, but as soon as such a form can be handled without losing shape, the center portion of the bottom may be pressed inward by hand or it may be repeatedly bumped with the anvil until the bottom is concave. The edge of the concave portion is the foot rim and should be kept level while you are working on the bottom. After you have scraped and sponged any sharp edges, the piece is ready to be dried slowly in a closed box, then fired.

FINISHING TOUCHES

Trim and round the rims of your coiled pieces by carefully trimming with the fettling knife

Non-symmetry may be developed by paddling as soon as clay will not stick to paddle.

Template useful to control large forms, mandatory for matching pieces.

and rounding with a wet sponge—rounded edges hold a glaze better than sharp edges.

All but the smallest coiled forms should have a foot rim. The foot functions as a protective feature and is an advantage when the piece is glost fired. Wait until the piece is leather-hard to make the foot. Then invert it and pencil a circle on the bottom, making area between circle and rim of piece match that of wall thickness. Use a wooden modeling tool and hollow the area within the circle to lower it about $\frac{1}{8}''$ for the piece 3" across, $\frac{3}{16}''$ for the 6", and $\frac{1}{4}''$ for the 9".

Some of your coiled pieces will require lids, handles or spouts—perhaps all three. These should be made of the same clay and at about the same time as the body of the piece is made. Attach handles and spouts when body is leather-hard.

HANDLES

To make a coil handle, use medium-stiff clay and roll coil of desired size. Cut to length and taper ends by pinching between thumb and forefinger. Bend and shape it carefully. Scratch surfaces where handle will meet pot and moisten with a paste made of thick clay. Press ends in place, weld and seal joints with added bits of clay for strength.

The pulled handle should be made from relatively stiff clay. Wedge the clay thoroughly and pat it into a pear-shaped wad. Grasp the large end of the wad of clay in the left hand with the small end pointing down. Lubricate the right hand with water and "milk" the small pointed end, pulling it into a long tapered strip of the desired shape and size. Pinch the handle from the wad and apply it to the form; the heavy end is the top of the handle. Some people prefer to shape it after pulling and permit it to harden to leather-hard on a plaster bat before applying. Weld it fast and seal the top of both joints with small cigar-shaped fillets of clay.

To make a slab handle, pat on back of oilcloth a slab of clay slightly greater in thickness than the wall of the container. Cut a slab from the pancake the desired width for a handle. Shape and apply the slab to the leather-hard form, sealing the top of each joint with a small cigar-shaped fillet of clay. When the handle is leather-hard, sponge and round all edges.

SPOUTS

Spouts can be made of short coils added directly to the form or built separately and welded in place on the piece as described in attaching handles. Cut container wall away inside spout and seal edges.

The pulled spout is most commonly used on pitchers. The spout should be pulled as soon as the form is completed, while the clay is still plastic. Support the top part of the wall on the outside with the thumb and first finger of the left hand held 1½ to 2″ apart. Using the first finger of the right hand, press the clay out between the thumb and finger of the left hand, as shown in the photographs in Chapter 9.

The slab spout can best be developed by cutting paper patterns. (See photographs in Chapter 9.) Select the pattern which is most suited to the form. Roll out or pat out a slab of clay of the desired thickness. Place the pattern on the clay slab and cut through the slab around the edge of the pattern with a fettling knife. Apply the spout to the form as shown in the photos in Chapter 9.

COVERS

If your piece is to have a cover, you must first decide if it will be a flanged one, whether it will rest on a rim inside the wall or on top of it.

Inside lid.

Lid with flange.

Outside lid.

In any case, check pot rim for roundness as soon as it is completed, pressing it gently with the hands to perfect any irregularities. If pot is to have an inside lid, first weld a coil inside to form a ledge. Distance from pot rim to top of ledge should equal wall thickness of pot. Next, pat out a clay pancake of this same thickness and cut a circle from it to equal diameter of pot opening minus ⅛″. When clay circle and pot are both leather-hard, add a modeled knob or coil loop to lid and sponge and fit it to the pot.

To make a cover with a flange, cut clay circle of same thickness as that of the pot's wall and

Pitcher with pulled spout, coil handle.

Pitcher with slab spout, pulled handle.

Horse fashioned from coils can be glazed
in imaginative, unhorselike color.

COILED FIGURES

Small, but highly decorative, figures are easy
to make with coils. Try your hand at making
a horse like that illustrated and it will lead you
toward making other figures of people or animals of your own design.

Start by making a length of coil about ⅝″ in
diameter. Cut two pieces approximately 4½″
long from this and press pieces together at the
center as you hold them parallel. Weld joint
about 1½″ long at center to make a solid oval
section for horse's body; the four free ends of
coil will be his legs. Gently bend the section to
form an arch and stand it on a tile or plaster
bat.

Next, cut a 2¼″ coil for the neck. Flatten ½″
at one end. Moisten this flat end and an end of
the body portion and weld together. In welding parts of figures, joints must be sealed to
prevent air from coming between them; air
causes them to separate during drying or
firing.

The head is made by rolling another 2¼″
length of coil to make an egg-shaped ball.
Pinch the neck to taper it and, after moistening both neck end and large end of the egg
shape, weld them together. Make and add eyes
and nostrils by rolling and flattening small
clay balls about the size of dried peas. A 1″
length of coil will make a tail, and two small
cigar-shaped wads the ears. Add a mane, if
you like, made with small clay loops, balls or
buttons.

When all parts are assembled, the fun of giv-
ing the figure expression can begin. Do this
while clay is still plastic and you can arch,
bend or turn neck and head to make your
horse look shy, inquisitive or surprised. At the
same time, separate the legs and place the
feet in desired positions.

After the figure has dried and been biscuit-
fired, consider glazing it in an imaginative,
although unhorselike, color. Make him pink,
yellow or blue, for instance, and he will truly
be a "horse of a different color."

equal in size to the outside diameter of pot's
opening. To locate position of the flange, sub-
tract wall thickness plus ⅟₁₆″ from edge of
clay circle. Using dividers, draw this smaller
circle on the clay. Make a coil and weld it in
position just inside scribed outline. When both
piece and lid are leather-hard, add knob to lid
and sponge to fit it to the pot.

The outside lid is made by cutting a clay circle
which is equal in size to the opening diameter
of the pot plus twice wall thickness and an
added ³⁄₁₆″. When clay is cut, add two coils
around and on top of the circle as in building
cylinder, welding them firmly in place. Add
knob, if desired, when lid and piece are leather-
hard. In fitting a lid of this type, allow from
⅛″ to ³⁄₁₆″ play between pot and lid.

When shaping of lid, of whatever type, is finished, let lid and pot dry as separate units.
For the best fit, however, biscuit-fire with lid
in place on pot.

40

1. Cut two pieces of coil 4½″ long.

2. Hold parallel and press center together.

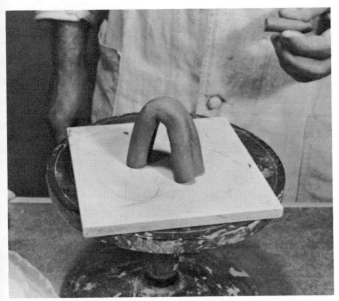

3. Gently bend to form arch, set on bat.

4. Add neck by welding moistened piece of coil.

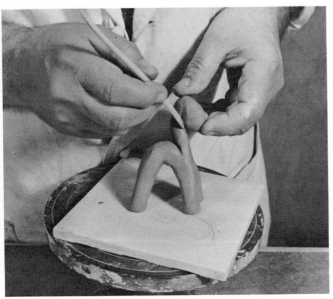

5. Egg-shaped pellet welded to neck for head.

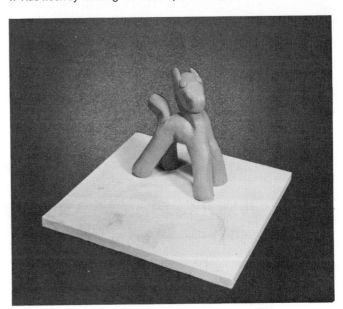

6. With all parts assembled, give personality to horse.

MARVIN WAX

Precise sophisticated planter made from slabs, and a slab piece that was paddled after building.

6 · Building with Slabs

The making of tiles and the constructing of forms from flat sheets of clay use a pottery technique which has been developed over many centuries. Excavations made in Egypt and Assyria have resulted in finds of tile murals of monumental proportions, and a study of the architecture of Spain, Turkey and Persia will show a generous use of tiles in these countries.

Almost any clay can be used in the making of tiles and slab wares. The fine-grained clays do tend to warp when used in these ways, however, and are improved by the addition of grog (20 to 40 mesh). Earthenware clays with grog added are readily available, or you can add grog to the clay you are using. Add ten or fifteen percent of red grog to white clay to make a good slab-building body—with an interesting speckled effect.

Beginners and experienced potters both enjoy using this method because it makes the forming of geometrically shaped wares a direct and easy process. You can make tiles, boxes with or without lids, flower pots, planters, bowls and straight-sided vases, lamp bases and innumerable other useful pieces with this simple technique. Cylindrical pieces can also be made with slabs—providing the curved wall does not exceed 2″ to 3″ in height.

MAKING TILES

To make tiles singly or by the dozens, you will need a length of oilcloth to stretch over the work table, a wooden rolling pin, two guide sticks (about 18″ long and as thick as tiles are to be) and a fettling knife.

Put oilcloth over table with the cloth side up and place mass of wedged clay on it. With guide sticks on two sides of the mass, roll clay as you would dough until the whole portion is exactly as thick as the guide sticks.

Mark out squares with ruler and pencil. These may be any size, but tiles are most often made in 4″ or 6″ squares. If exact finished size is important, allow a margin of about ⅛″ for shrinkage.

When tile dimensions are marked and while clay is still soft, use fettling knife to cut it through for about one-half its thickness. Make light cuts. Do not allow knife to drag and distort tile edges. Edges will also become distorted if clay is completely cut through at this stage.

After an hour or two, clay will have stiffened to cheese-like consistency and cutting of tile outlines can be completed. Smooth edges with a wet sponge.

If you are using a grogged clay, tiles can usually be dried on an open shelf if turned over every two or three hours during the first day's drying. If tiles are made of a fine-grained clay which tends to warp, turn them over after sponging edges and cut grooves in the back to a depth of about one-third of tile thickness. This will minimize warping.

Tiles may be dried on wire screen or sandwiched between 8″ plaster bats, but they must lie flat in both the drying and firing periods.

Tiles frequently use decorative treatments given before they are completely dry. For suggestions concerning the decorating of tiles see Chapter 8.

SLAB PLATES

Making a set of square plates is an interesting project, and the resulting dishes should be an attractive addition to your collection of table ware. Circular plates can also be made from slabs, but they are more difficult to form satisfactorily—the circular form is likely to be irregular, the flared edge uneven.

Decorative tiles call for good design sense.

Equipment needed is the same as that used in making tiles. In addition, you'll require a paper pattern cut to the shape and size of the plate desired.

To make the pattern for the plate illustrated, fold an 8″ square of paper in quarters, folding this quarter square once again. Trim point to round corners of the square. Finished plate will be smaller than pattern due to clay shrinkage during drying and firing.

To make a plate, wedge about 1½ pounds of medium-stiff clay and pat it into a ball. Flatten and roll out with rolling pin and guide sticks to make slab ¼″ thick.

Lay paper pattern on the clay and cut around pattern outline with large pin, darning needle or point of the fettling knife. Remove excess clay and allow slab to set until it can be moved without misshaping it.

When stiff enough to handle, move slab to a plaster bat large enough to support it in its entirety. Roll coils ½″ in diameter and use these to raise the edges of the slab to give plate a gently curved rim. Let the plate stand with edges held up by the supporting coils until it is leather-hard. Then remove coils and trim plate edges with knife or a wire-ended

KENNETH DIERCK

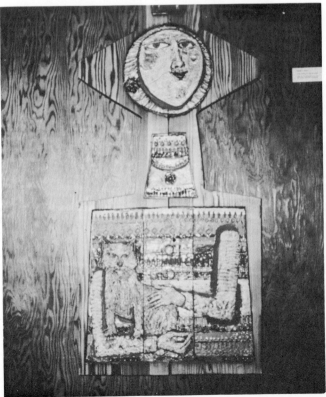

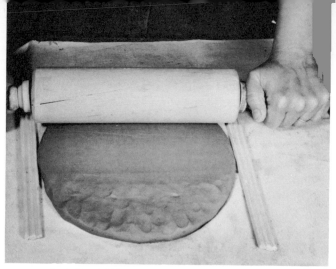

1. Roll out 1½ pounds clay to quarter-inch slab.

2. Cut out clay following paper pattern.

3. Place supporting coil under edge.

4. Trim edges of leather-hard plate with tool.

5. Apply glaze to biscuited plate with brush.

6. Finished, fired plate graces patio table.

PAULA PALMER

modeling tool as shown in the accompanying illustration. Finish smoothing of rim with a wet sponge.

To keep it from warping, plate should dry slowly. Set it on a damp plaster bat and cover with a damp cloth. Remove cloth after 24 hours and set plate away to dry completely before biscuit-firing.

SLAB BOXES

Procedures for rolling slabs to make box forms are the same as those used in making tiles. Patterns of paper or light cardboard will be useful in cutting matching rectangles for sides, ends, etc. Allow cut clay parts to become leather-hard before attempting to build with them.

All joints in the form must be well sealed or they may split during drying or firing. To make good joints, first wet edges with "slip." Slip, in this instance, is a thin cream made of your clay and water. Apply two coats with a soft brush. After pressing slip-coated joints together, work them solidly into position with a slight rocking motion. If clay is at all dry, make light scored cuts in the edges before applying slip and joining edges. Joints can be further strengthened and rounded by adding a small coil along inside angles, pressing it along adjoining angles. Seal and weld outside joints with wooden modeling tool. For best results, set box walls on top of the base, not around it.

When box is leather-hard, round edges and outside corners and set it away to dry.

The addition of a well-designed foot and cover will turn a simple box form into an attractive container. To make a foot, invert box (after it is leather-hard) and add slab strips as shown in the photographs illustrating the making of the flared slab bowl.

Lids can be fitted to rest inside the box opening, to rest on top of the box walls or to cover them. Types of lids are illustrated and de-scribed on pages discussing the coiled form. Lids for the rectangular box are made by cutting clay rectangles from slabs and fitting them with knobs, flanges, etc.

SLAB BOWL WITH FLARED SIDES

To make a bowl of this type you will need the slab-making equipment previously described and a paper pattern made by folding a rectangle and cutting a narrow, triangular notch from the corner. The bowl pictured is 6" x 7½".

Lay pattern on prepared slab of clay and cut around it. Remove excess and, when the flat form is stiff enough to lift, score edges of corner joints by making small incisions along cut edges with a knife. Work thin slip into incisions with a soft brush. To make corner joint, pinch seams firmly together from the outside. Support newly formed corner with a brick or a section of a wood 2" x 4", then join and support other corners. Seal corner joints with clay taken from both sides and pushed into the angle with the wooden modeling tool. Cover completed bowl with a damp cloth and let it set until leather-hard.

As soon as the bowl can be safely handled, invert and make foot measurements. Mark a line along all four sides of the bottom to act as

To make sure that box parts will fit, make accurate, squared patterns from cardboard and cut matching clay forms with knife.

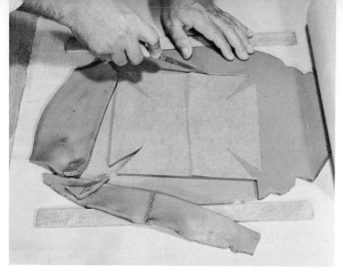

1. Cut around paper pattern, discard excess.

2. Pinch corners together, support with bricks.

3. Attach foot strips to incised lines with slip.

4. Weld foot to bottom with modeling tool.

5. Round leather-hard edges with sponge.

6. Finished piece ready to be biscuit-fired.

guide for locating position of strips which make the foot. Roll out slab of the same thickness as the bowl—¼″ for bowl shown—and cut four strips ½″ wide and approximately the length of the bowl. Cut these to length after they have stiffened.

While strips stiffen, make small incisions in the clay of the bowl bottom just inside outlines marked for the foot. Next cut the long side pieces to exact length of the marked area and the short end pieces to a measure ½″ shorter than the width of the area. Ends fit between sides when joined on bowl bottom.

To add foot, first score edges of side strips and ½″ of inside surface at ends. Wet scored edges of these and the matching sections on bowl bottom with water or thin slip and press together with slight rocking motion to join securely.

Prepare end strips by scoring one edge and both ends of each and join to bowl in the same manner. Weld all joints solidly on inside and outside. Round inside corners with modeling tool by drawing a little clay from bowl to strip. On the inside of the foot, add extra clay at joint by pressing a small coil or "fillet" into adjoining angles.

Set inverted bowl away in a closed box or cupboard for twelve hours. Moisture in bowl and foot will have equalized in that time and you can then round all of the edges with a modeling tool and wet sponge. Be sure to allow the bowl to dry completely before firing.

LARGE SLAB FORMS

When you have discovered the various ways to handle the partially stiffened slabs and the means by which they may be joined together, you are ready to experiment with unusual shapes of larger size. Such large slab forms can follow many patterns and have many variations. Like the smaller forms, they should be carefully planned before you begin any actual clay working.

Probably the greatest problems in making

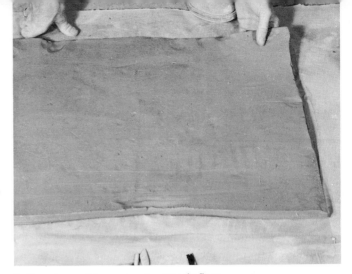

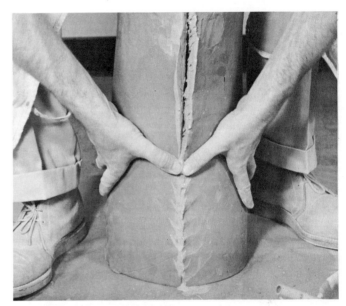

1. Form large slabs on garage or patio floor.

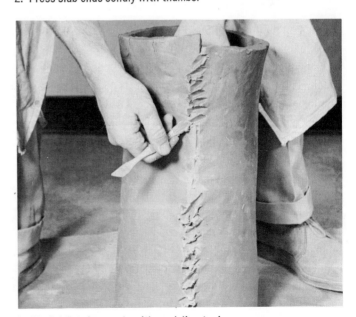

2. Press slab ends solidly with thumbs.

3. Work joint vigorously with modeling tool.

4. Cut top of base to contour of drum.

5. Paddle top of base to line up with drum.

6. Weld solidly, then reinforce with clay coil.

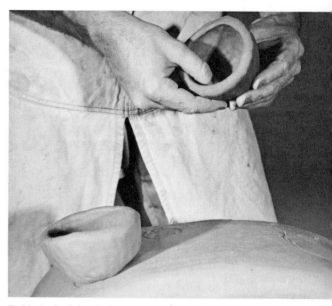

7. Mark pinch-bowl placement on drum.

8. Score, add slip, and attach pinch bowls.

9. Paddle to insure solid joint.

large forms, aside from that of actually handling large quantities of clay and keeping it together, is finding sufficient space to roll out good-sized slabs. A patio or garage floor may alleviate this situation. However, if the patio is used, try to avoid working clay in the hot sun.

The oval drum by Philip Cornelius (see pages 47, 48) is 28″ high, over-all. For large slab forms, wall thickness is most important for strength. In the drum, the flat surfaces are ½″ slabs separated by a ¾″ slab. The assembled drum is 8″ wide, 12″ high, and 16″ long; the supporting base, made from a ¾″ slab, is 16″ high.

To make the drum, prepare paper patterns for all parts except the pinched spouts. Roll out ½″ slab for the drum faces and ¾″ slab for a separator. Place an oval pattern on the drum face slabs and mark around it with pencil but do not cut the slabs. Set the face slabs and separator aside to harden slightly while you roll out and cut a ¾″ slab for the cylindrical base.

Return to the drum and check the slabs for hardness; the ¾″ slab should still be plastic but should be able to support itself when stood on edge. Score the face slabs, making ⅛″ deep and 1″ long incisions with the point of wooden modeling tool inside the pencil-marked ovals. Score all edges of ¾″ separator slab in the same way, and give all scored areas a liberal coating of thick slip. Assemble the separator on one drum face and work it solidly into position with a slight rocking motion. Slip should form a bead both inside and outside the joint. Press the ends of the separator slab solidly together with your thumbs, and work them vigorously together with tip of modeling tool. Then reinforce the joint with coil both inside and outside. Weld the coil into position, then paddle flat.

Cut the top drum face from slab ¼″ outside the oval pencil line. Place the top face slab in

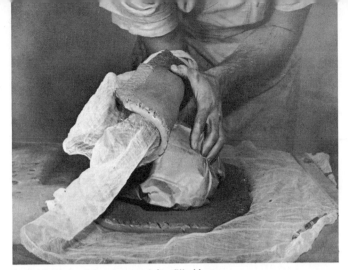

1. Fold single slab over excelsior-filled bag.

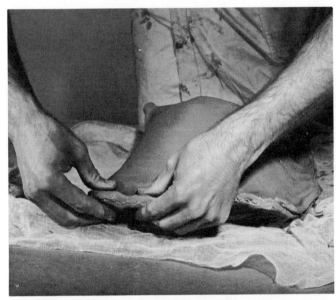

2. Pinch scored and slip-coated edges solidly.

3. Cheesecloth provides sling for support.

position, and press the joint firmly together until a bead of slip appears entirely around oval. If bead does not appear, paddle gently until it does. Permit the drum to harden, and then assemble cylindrical base as above.

As soon as drum is hardened enough to hold its shape when lifted, paddle ¼" surplus over the edge of separator rounding edge. Cut through bottom face slab, leaving ¼" surplus, turn the drum over, and paddle surplus over the edge as you did on other side. Assemble drum on base by cutting top of base to contour of drum. Score surfaces to be joined, apply slip, and place drum in position. If base extends beyond drum, lift drum slightly and paddle top of base until it lines up as desired. Press drum firmly into position, and weld solidly to base, reinforcing with clay coil. Invert assembled form and reinforce inside joint also.

Now pinch out a number of varied sizes of small bowls and check them for size and shape on top of drum. Select those to be used, and mark out their placement on drum. Cut bottom from the bowls, score, add slip, and attach them to drum separator. A paddle may be used to insure solid joints. Cut through drum separator inside spouts and remove the cutout area. Work all joints firmly together.

An applique decoration is optional. If desired, you may use thin slabs, score, slip, and paddle them to the surface. Permit the form to become leather hard, then do any smoothing with a damp sponge and modeling tool.

IRREGULAR SLAB FORMS

The large irregular form by Joe Hawley (pages 49, 50, 51) combines slab and thrown forms in a most unusual and interesting manner. The body of such a piece may be quite varied in form and offers a great deal of opportunity for creative imagination.

In making this irregular form, a ⅜" thick rectangular slab was rolled out on a piece of

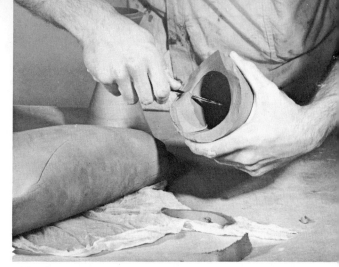

4. Cut top edge of base on taper to fit curve.

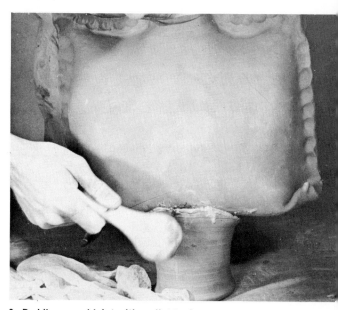

6. Paddle curved joint with mallet tool.

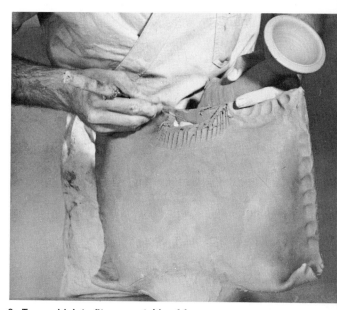

8. Tapered joints fit over outside of form.

5. Score and slip-coat form and base.

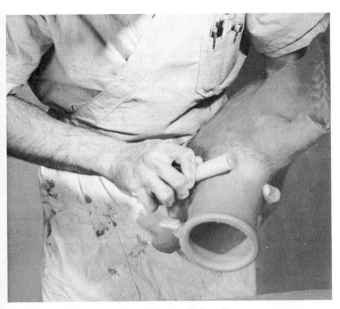

7. Weld joint with fettling knife handle.

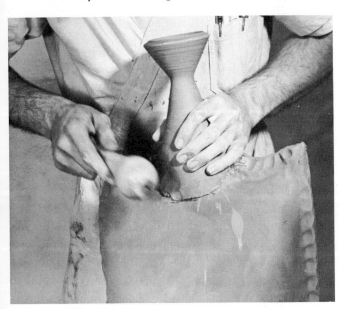

9. Paddle tapered, scored, slip-coated neck joint.

cheesecloth, and the edges were immediately scored and coated with thick slip. Then a paper bag filled with excelsior was placed on half of the single slab, and the other half was folded over so that the edges matched. (The bag and excelsior burn out on firing.) As the edges were solidly pinched together, body contour was formed. The cheesecloth was then folded over the form to provide a supporting sling, and the cloth was suspended by clamping the top edges between two boards in a vise.

The cylindrical base and conical neck were then thrown, and all parts were permitted to become leather hard. The form was then removed from the sling, and joining parts of the base and neck were cut and pressed to the contour of the form. The joining surfaces were scored, coated with slip, placed in position, and worked vigorously together. A wooden weeding tool with metal prongs removed was used as a paddle for curved surfaces, and the handle of a fettling knife was used as a modeling tool where strong pressure was necessary. Joining edges of the foot and neck were cut on taper to fit over the outside of the form before attaching.

Irregular slab forms show variety, imagination.

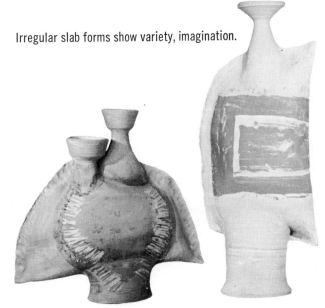

JOE HAWLEY

DRAPE MOLD. 1. Place mold on top of slab.

MOLDED SLABS

Matching sets of bowls for serving popcorn, soup, salad and other foods are easily made by molding soft slabs in or over forms. When form used is hollow and the clay slab smoothed and pushed into it, it is known as a "press mold." The inside of the mold forms the outside of the pottery piece. Another type of mold used with slabs is the "drape mold." This is a convex shape and the slab is draped and smoothed over it to form the piece. In this case the outside of the mold forms the inside of the pot. Drape-molded forms will be most successful if pieces are made rather shallow.

MAKING A PRESS MOLD

Build this type of mold with thick coils unless it is to be quite small—small forms can be shaped by pinching. The main requirement of the press mold is that it be free from bumps and irregularities on the inner surface. A foot can be carved directly in the mold bottom if desired. Foot curves should be gradual and easy, without sharp angles or corners which would not allow clay to move as it dries and shrinks. Foot rims can also be added to the outside of the press-molded form after it is leather-hard.

When the coiled or pinched form is completely dry, fire it to a dull red heat to make it durable for use.

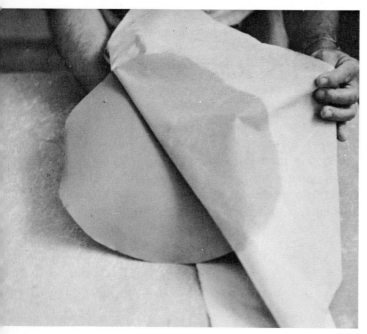

2. Turn over, peel off oilcloth.

MAKING A DRAPE MOLD

Making the drape or "hump" mold, as it is sometimes called, is actually a problem in modeling. Model a mound of clay to the desired form. Smooth by sponging molding surface. The underside of the form may be hollowed to a mushroom-like form if desired, although this is not necessary. Do hollowing after clay is leather-hard. When mold is completely dry, fire to a dull red heat to fit it for use.

3. Press to form, trim edge, smooth with sponge.

USING THE MOLDS

Use any clay for either drape or press molding. Since clay must be shaped over or in the mold while still plastic, roll slabs out on a piece of cloth or canvas which you can lift with the slab on it. Invert cloth and clay over the form and lower it. Peel away cloth and press clay into position either in or on mold, starting at mold center. The prime objective in molding is to achieve a bowl wall uniformly thick throughout. Variation in thickness may cause piece to warp or crack.

In smoothing walls, use the wooden modeling tool to scrape away bumps and uneven spots and the dampened sponge to smooth them. Remove excess clay from around rims with knife and smooth with sponge. As soon as clay is leather-hard and has shrunk to cause it to pull away from the mold, it can be removed from mold.

To remove piece from a press mold, place a plaster bat on top of mold and invert. Lift mold and sponge and round pot rim. Add a foot, if one is desired and not formed by the inside of the mold, made of strip or coil.

If the drape-molded shape is to have a foot, add it while form is still supported by the mold. When all parts of the piece are leather-hard, lift it from the mold to finish drying.

BOX MOLDS

Large straight-sided pots, planters or lamp bases can be more easily made of clay slabs if these are supported by a box-like arrangement of boards. Make a four-sided box with open ends and inside dimensions equal to outside dimensions required for the piece. If two corners of the box mold are solidly fastened and the other two joined by lapping and nailing—nails driven in only part way—the form is easy to remove by simply pulling the nails on the two lapped corners.

Form the large straight-sided pieces by pressing slabs inside the mold, which has been set

PRESS MOLD. 1. Place slab in mold.

2. Pat into place, trim excess.

3. Smooth inside surface with sponge.

1. Cut bear from doubled paper pattern.

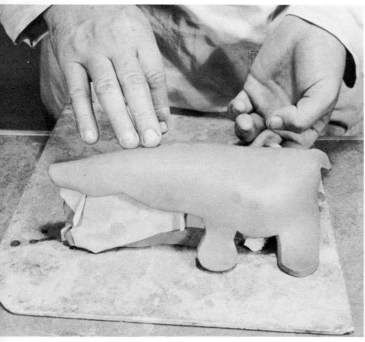

2. Form figure by draping around tapered clay wad.

3. Finished product glazed in cream, appropriate for polar bear. Triangular ears attached with slip.

on a plaster bat large enough to accommodate the bottom. Round and strengthen joints at inside angles with fillets made of clay coils. Trim the rim level with the top edge of mold.

If piece is to be a plant container, cut a small drainage hole in the bottom. If it is to be a lamp base, make a small hole above the bottom on one side for the cord and add a top slab with any necessary openings for lamp fittings cut in it.

As soon as clay stiffens and shrinks to pull away from the wooden form, remove the form. Use wet sponge to round corners and edges, then set the piece away on supporting bat until it is completely dry. Large pieces should dry slowly, so cover with damp cloth for 24 hours at the start of the drying period.

SLAB SCULPTURE

You'll find the making of small sculptures by this method both entertaining and easy. Results can be amusing and decorative, too. The method is a simple one—slab is cut to a pattern and the figure rounded and draped over a temporary support. As a beginning, you may want to use the pattern for the polar bear given here. You can, of course, develop your own patterns to make original figures.

To make the bear, first cut out a doubled paper pattern. Lay it on a slab about 1/4″ thick which has been rolled on cloth which can be lifted. Prepare a support by making a tapered wad of clay about 3″ high or use a small glass jar laid on its side in a wad of clay to keep it from rolling. Cover either type of support with paper toweling so slab will not stick to it.

Cut clay around pattern with the knife. Remove excess clay and allow form to stiffen slightly. Then place plaster bat on top of clay and turn bat, clay and cloth over as one. Lift off bat and peel cloth from clay. Use both hands to lift it and drape it over the prepared form. Bend sides, feet and head to shape them. If neck shows a tendency to droop, support head with a temporary clay post.

When bear is leather-hard, add ears made of small triangles, joining them to head with slip. Press in place and smooth joints with modeling tool.

When bear can stand alone, remove him from the support and sponge and round all edges.

Animals in sitting positions, or those with humped or curved backs, are better depicted as slab sculptures when they are made with patterns and slabs cut in two pieces. The engaging little squirrel shown here is an example of this type of form.

To make the squirrel according to the pattern given here, start with about 3½ pounds of medium-stiff wedged clay. Roll out slab and cut out two matching squirrel shapes. While these stiffen to allow handling, prepare a tapered clay plug 4″ high, with diameters of 1½″ at the bottom and ¾″ at top.

When clay shapes can be lifted safely, assemble by placing one on either side of the upright plug. Pinch the edges of the two slabs together from the nose to the ears. Do not pinch ears together—bend them outward instead. Pinch edges of body along neck and line next to tail. Pinch top edges of tail together; let the figure set for about an hour. Then shape tail, head, legs and body. When squirrel is leather-hard, remove plug and seal all inside joints with modeling tool. Round edges with damp sponge and set piece away to dry.

1. Duplicate halves cut from paper pattern.

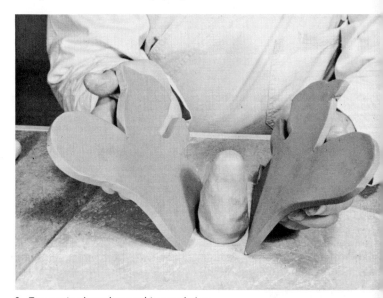

2. Two parts shaped around tapered plug.

3. Completed squirrel formed by pinching edges of two slabs together, allowing clay to set, then shaping tail, head, body.

Cut out doubled paper pattern

56

Cut two matching shapes

Figures made of ceramic clays should be bold and simple, free of details.

7 · Ceramic Sculpture

This phase of working with clay is the most fascinating of all to many people. Since the shaping of clay to make figures is such an integral part of the ceramic processes, methods of making small ones by pinching, coiling and slab modeling have been included in chapters on building by these methods. Methods and means of making larger sculptures are considered here.

Clay for sculpture usually contains a fairly high proportion of reasonably coarse grog. Inclusion of grog does several things. It adds texture which is often desirable when the piece is large and clay is not to be covered with glaze. Clay color can be made more in-

teresting in some cases by using grog of a color contrasting to that of the clay body. If surface of the sculpture is to be smooth but not glazed, it can be sponged lightly with an elephant-ear sponge when nearly dry to bring out grog color. Emery cloth or sandpaper may be used to smooth surface after firing. Addition of grog opens clay structure to make it more porous which helps in drying and firing and also enables it to take up water readily if work must be moistened during modeling.

Exact amounts of grog to add will depend on the effects desired and can be determined only by individual experiment. Up to 25 percent may be added, however, without destroying

57

plastic quality of clay needed for sculptural purposes.

Clay sculptures will be best if expressed in compact forms fittingly designed for the material. It has been said that any sculpture should be formed so it can roll down hill—extended limbs or appendages would break off with such treatment—and while it is hardly advisable to so treat any ceramic piece, it is suggested that you plan to keep sculpture features tucked in rather than extended.

The most used method in modeling sculpture is that of building up the main masses with small wads of clay. The whole figure is solidly built and roughly modeled to shape over the entire form. Refining of details is done when clay has stiffened slightly. When solid pieces of any size are leather-hard they should be cut in half and halves hollowed until walls are fairly uniform in thickness. The hollowed halves are then moistened at edges, covered with slip and rejoined. If openings do not comprise a part of the design, drill or pierce one or two small holes in the bottom to serve as air vents needed when piece is fired. Pieces which set flat on the table may be hollowed from the bottom and need not be cut in half.

Quite small figures (those 3″ to 4″ in diameter), or those slightly larger which have had careful building and complete and slow drying, are often successfully fired without being hollowed. If much such solid modeling is to be done, it is advisable to do the drying in a pottery drier (a closed cabinet with a means of maintaining a constant temperature of from 150 to 175 degrees F.).

The small doe pictured is an example of modeling done solidly and subsequently hollowed. The basic form was developed roughly from a single mound of red-firing, grogged clay of coarse texture. An upright column for the neck and knob for the head were squeezed from one end of the mound. Legs were also modeled from the mound mass. Ears and tail were modeled, and surfaces finished, when the clay had stiffened somewhat but was not yet leather-hard. When leather-hard, body mound and neck were hollowed from the bottom and head left solid. The finished figure, 10½″ high and 12″ long, is glazed in cream color glaze of a semi-matte surface.

Coil-built figures are built hollow. The main masses of the figure are made as coiled shapes with each coil welded inside and out as building progresses. Refinements and additions to the form are made when clay has stiffened but is not yet leather-hard.

There is, of course, a tremendous variety in what can be done with coil-built sculpture. Animals, human figures, abstract decorative figures, and utilitarian objects of various sizes can be made. The figures can be glazed or left unglazed. See the illustrated coil-built lantern and coil-built owl for two of many possibilities.

COIL-BUILT LANTERN

To build the bird-cage type of lantern shown, roll out several long lengths of coil about ⅝″ in diameter. Drape vertical coils over a sheet metal form, or use a clay hump covered with paper towel. Next, attach horizontal coils to the vertical ones, using slip. When leather hard, carefully remove cage from form and mount on a leather-hard slab. Reinforce with coil on top of slab. Add a looped-coil handle.

Foot-long figure of doe
was modeled as a solid,
hollowed out when stiff.

PINCH SCULPTURE

Interesting and decorative sculpture can be made by the pinch process. The animal on the next page, by John Leary, is particularly appealing. To make, pinch a bowl with greater thickness at rim than throughout wall of form. When bowl is desired size, squeeze it so that the edges of rim come together. Do not flatten form. Weld edges and smooth the joint. Do necessary shaping and set aside to become leather hard. Make legs, score, and attach to form with slip. Press legs firmly into position, weld joints, and do any final shaping. Paddle lightly for subtlety of form. Incise eyes and decoration, paint, and dry-brush colored slip over back. Sculpture from red or brown clays is often left unglazed.

SLAB SCULPTURE

A decorative household guardian by John Leary doubles as a candle sconce. The highly abstract figure with a small, double-pinched bowl head has a face in back as well as in front, thus watches both back and front doors at same time. (See page 61.)

Roll a rectangular slab to ½" thickness and cut to desired size. Lightly sketch an arc at one end of rectangle, using point of fettling knife or a lead pencil. Cut through slab and remove arc. Use arc as base for figure. Drape oilcloth and slab over a cylindrical form—a rolling pin or a glass jar will serve. When leather hard, score joints, coat with slip, and assemble as for other slab pieces. Attach pinched candle holder and double pinched head. Coat form with wax, incise through the wax, and paint over incising with different colored slips. Sculpture is left unglazed.

THE THROWN PADDLED FIGURE

The variations possible in thrown sculpture are virtually unlimited. See, in Chapter 9, how wheel sculpture can retain the quality of thrown forms. The illustrations in the left column on page 62 show how Claude Horan retains qualities characteristic of the wheel in a thrown then paddled sculpture.

JOHN LEARY

Coil-built lantern stands on flat surface or can be hung by chain.

FRED HAMILTON

Coil-built owl has stylized face and body. Texture is made with fettling tool.

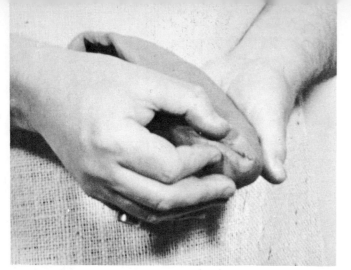

PINCH SCULPTURE. 1. Squeeze edges of rim.

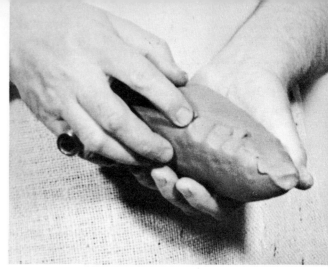

2. Weld the joint, holding form carefully.

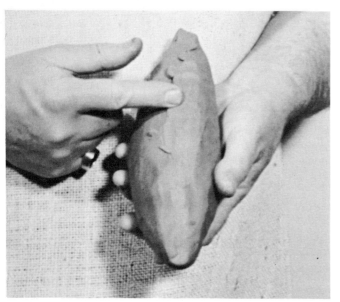

3. Smooth the joint, using fingers.

4. Roll legs and attach with slip.

JOHN LEARY

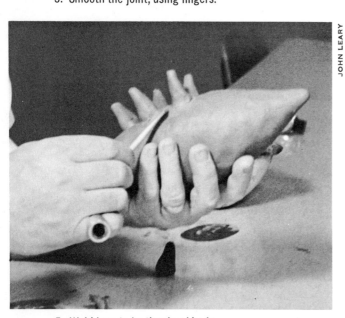

5. Weld legs to leather-hard body.

Eyes and decoration are incised,
and colored slip is brushed over back.

Candle holder waxed when leather hard, scratched, painted with colored slips, biscuit-fired high.

A more complex slab sculpture made from several pieces and glazed.

JOAN BUGBEE

JOHN LEARY

THE THROWN MODELED FIGURE

Maryann Gravitt does not paddle her sculpture but models from both inside and outside, accenting modeled areas by cutting through the wall and by adding portions of the figure as slabs. The second series of photographs on page 62 explains the process.

MODELING TOOLS

As always, fingers are the first tools in these clay-shaping techniques. There are several tools you may want to add to your equipment. Modeling tools are available with wires shaped

61

THROWN PADDLED FIGURE. 1. Detail with paddle handle.

THROWN MODELED FIGURE. 1. Arm outline cut through.

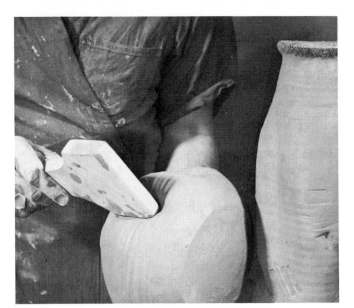

2. Side of paddle develops head features.

2. Arm brought forward and body pressed together.

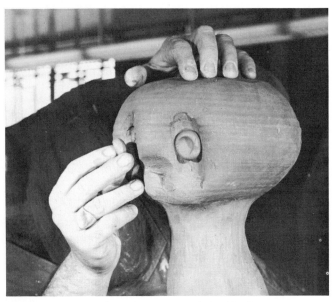

3. Balls of clay for eyes attached with slip.

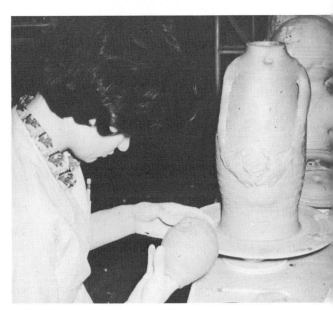

3. Head is modeled and attached to body.

Coil-built bird
with applied decoration.
Purple brown matte glaze.

to make loops of various forms at end of the wooden handles and with loops made of metal strips, as well as knives and wooden modeling tools in numerous shapes and sizes. Choose from these according to your needs, but strive to use the largest tool compatible with the work to avoid small and niggling effects.

GENERAL SUGGESTIONS

Principles in making sculpture of clay are the same as those in making such forms in any other sculptural medium in most regards. Although the aesthetics of the matter are outside the scope of this book, the following suggestions should be of help in handling clay to make sculptured forms.

Start the figure on a base large enough to hold it and place so you can turn the work continually. Work around the entire figure, developing detail at about the same rate all over it, rather than concentrating on a detail which might later prove to be misplaced. Turning

and working around the piece will enable you to see it three-dimensionally. Add moist clay to moist clay surfaces to build and fasten clay parts. If some part of the figure proves to have been over-built, cut off a little more clay than is needed, bringing it to an under-built stage, and then replace clay until the amount is right. Bear in mind that building is adding clay—not pushing, pulling or rubbing it from one place to another. The finished shape should look as if it had been made of clay.

If figure is to be glazed (large ones are often left unglazed), this should be taken into account in the designing. The dull, matte glazes are usually preferred, because the non-reflecting surfaces allow planes to be seen without the visual confusion often present when highly reflecting, shiny glazes are used. Small figures are occasionally accented with sections of enamel-like opaque glaze on a background of unglazed clay body color, or wholly covered for various decorative effects.

Stoneware cylinders with
incised decoration,
willow wood ash glaze.

8 · Decorative Processes

Surface decoration can be added to the pottery form in many ways. Decoration of the form may be thought of first, perhaps, as a coating of glaze, appropriate in color and kind to fit both the shape and its ultimate use. Glazes in many colors are also used to paint designs or patterns chosen to produce certain textures and effects, and for other forms of embellishment. Since glazing is a foremost means of pottery decoration an entire section of this chapter is devoted to the process. There are, however, a number of other ways of adding decorations to the surface of your wares which you will want to consider.

The matter of adding surface decoration to a pottery form must be decided upon according to individual preference. You are the potter—the choice is yours. As skills develop, you will find a tendency to think of pottery forms as finished realities—complete with planned decorative effects. In the meantime, you can experiment with a few basic decorating processes. A number of these are described here. Use tiles or clay slabs as "sketch pads"—these can be fired, glazed and filed away for ready reference. You might, for instance, make several 4″ or 6″ tiles and make samplers of the various processes to be described. After biscuit-firing your samplers, apply various glazes in parallel stripes across each tile and then glost-fire them so you can see both glaze colors and how they appear when used with these particular techniques.

IMPRESSED DECORATION

Almost any familiar object can be used to impress texture or pattern in damp clay surfaces.

Use the end of your wooden modeling tool, a pebble, the edge of an apricot pit or a piece of coarsely woven cloth or matting. You can, if you like, design decorative motifs and carve them in wood, plaster, clay or linoleum to make clay stamps. One such stamp might be designed as your personal "trade mark."

Impressed decoration can be added to your clay tile or slab as soon as it is hard enough to be picked up and turned over without losing shape. If it becomes too hard, it will crack or break when impressions are made. Tile can be brought back into condition for impressing by covering it with a dampened cloth for a few minutes. If impressed decorations are made on the outside of a pot, support the wall on the inside at point of impression with left hand.

CARVED DECORATIONS

Carved decorations may consist of incised or excised lines or areas, pierced areas made by removing clay completely, or a combination of all three forms of carving.

Incised decoration is made by carving the motif or pattern into the surface. Such carving lowers pattern, leaving background areas of the original clay thickness. Pattern may be linear or mass or a combination of line and mass. Any blunt point, such as that of a lead pencil or a bobby pin fastened to a stick, will make an incising tool for linear patterns. Large areas can be cut or scraped away with the loop end of the wire modeling tool or end of the knife blade. This technique should be practiced upon a medium-stiff leather-hard tile.

In excised decoration the background is lowered or carved into the clay surface to leave the elements forming the design motif at original levels. The lowered background may be left smooth or various textures may be impressed or incised into it. Tools used are the same as those used for incising and a medium-stiff tile should be used as a sampler.

Excised decoration is done when clay is leather hard.

Incising may become a texture. Here, outside of jar is unglazed.

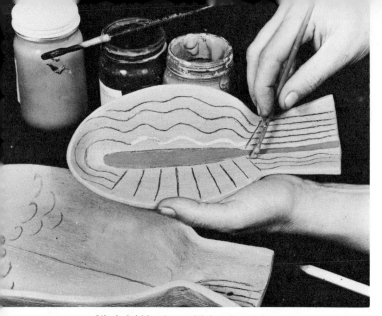

Slip is laid in place with brush, not drawn along clay. Clay should be leather-hard.

Eye-dropper or small syringe can be used to apply slip in lines, dots.

Colored slip can be incised to show clay color beneath: process called "sgraffito."

Pierced carving calls for removal of areas forming either motif or background. Clay for this type of carving must not be too stiff or it will crack and break during the process.

DECORATING WITH SLIP

Decorating slips are clays mixed with sufficient water to make them of thick-cream consistency. You can buy slips in many colors from your ceramic supply dealer, or, if the clay you are using fires white, cream or buff, you can add metallic oxides or stains according to the table given at the end of this chapter to make your own. Color ingredients should be thoroughly ground into slip with mortar and pestle and rubbed through an 80-mesh screen for use in decorating. Mortars and mesh screens are available at ceramic supply stores.

SLIP PAINTING

Slip may be applied with a brush on unfired, leather-hard pieces. Textural variations are achieved by using slip in thick or thin dilutions, by light or heavy application and with a dry brush technique. Brush painting on thirsty dried clay with slip will call for a different technique than other forms of brush painting. The dry clay draws moisture from the liquid slip at a rapid rate and slip is actually laid in place with the brush rather than drawn along with it as in enameling, for instance.

SLIP TRACING

This decorative process has been used on pottery made by the Romans, by the English, the Pennsylvania Dutch settlers in our own country and by European potters. The slip tracing cup was made of clay shaped to fit the hand with quills or tubes protruding from one side of the cup. As cup was held in the hand for use, tubes stuck out between fingers and the open top of the cup was covered by the palm of the hand. When palm was slightly lifted slip would flow through the tubes; when lowered, palm acted as a lid and stopped the flow of slip. You can, if you wish, make such a multiple-tubed cup. A rubber syringe, of the type used for ears or infant hygiene, will make a satisfactory substitute. Fill syringe with thick slip so no air is held in the bulb to cause slip to splash or splatter. Uniform and even pressure on the bulb as the tube is drawn along the lines of the motif should result in an even flow of slip. Do slip tracing on leather-hard clay.

SGRAFFITO

This is an Italian word meaning "scratched through" and the sgraffito form of pottery decoration is done by scratching a pattern through a slip coat to reveal clay body color underneath. Apply the coat of slip to leather-hard clay by brushing, dipping or spraying. Let slip dry until it no longer sticks to the fingers in handling and then scratch lines with blunt point of a lead pencil or a bobby pin and scrape areas with wire-ended modeling tool or knife point.

MISHIMA

This form of decoration was developed by the Koreans and named by the Japanese. Decorations on the first pieces embellished in this manner imported into Japan resembled the writing on the Japanese Almanac. Consequently, the name of this form of decoration means "Almanac writing."

Mishima decoration is made by first impressing, incising or excising the motif into the clay surface and then covering it with a thin coating of slip in a color to contrast with the clay body. When slip is no longer sticky, sponge or scrape it from raised portions of the design. A thin film of slip left on some of the raised areas serves to add interest to the textural quality. Try this on a portion of the excised, incised or impressed tile decorations.

STAMPED OR STIPPLED SLIP

Still another way to use slip is stippling it on leather-hard ware with a sponge. Add water

Red, gray, black bands of slip over surface, sgraffito through bands, gray semi-matt glaze.

Carved motifs decorate unglazed terra cotta.

Black glaze over ground of
white matt glaze.

Although one function of glaze is that of
beautification of the piece, another is that of
sealing the clay surface to make it more easily
cleaned and sanitary in use. This last is most
important in tableware and of little or no importance in other kinds of ware. A first consideration in the choice of the selection of
glaze for a particular piece might then be that
of function or appearance.

Again, the decoration of your pottery, this
time by the application of glaze, will be a matter of personal choice. There are many kinds
to choose from. Glazes may be colorless, adding a sealing coat over clay body color but
not concealing it; they may be colored and
transparent, opalescent, semi-transparent or
opaque. Most are glossy and highly reflecting. Some have matte or semi-matte surfaces,
these being dull or partially dulled and non-
reflecting.

In selecting a glaze, bear in mind that a glaze
brightly colored and highly glossy can be ap-
propriately used on a small bowl or vase, im-
parting a jewel-like elegance to it. The same
glaze might well prove inappropriate for a
larger form, making it only gaudy or vulgar.
Here, a matte glaze would perhaps have been
a better choice. These dull coatings are thick
and rather heavy; and while they look well on
massive pieces, they can overwhelm a smaller
piece and may completely obliterate any small
detail.

PURCHASING PREPARED GLAZES

Glazes are composed of powdered chemicals
and minerals which assume the positions of
bases, acids and neutrals in the total composition. Differences in color result from the addition of color-producing metallic oxides, either

to make a thinner than customary slip for this.
Thin slip can also be used with rubber stamps
on leather-hard or dry clay.

MODELED DECORATION

Modeling of applied clay shapes fastened to
tile or pot surface with slip can be done when
clay can be handled. Use the wooden modeling
tool to round the edges of applied motifs and
press them into place. Dry pieces with such
decorations very slowly, checking periodically
to see that applied shapes do not loosen.

GLAZING

Ceramic glazes are complex fusions which
have been classified as both solid solutions and
super-cooled liquids. Glazes and glazing will
be better understood by the beginner or hobbyist if he thinks of glazes simply as a coating
of glass which has fused to the surface of the
clay during the firing process.

Rough-textured stoneware with glaze decoration.

raw or as prepared stains. The study of glaze composition is one of the most fascinating in the whole ceramic field. As a budding potter, you will take advantage of the prepared glazes and glaze powders which you can purchase. Some simple experiments in making glazes are given later in this chapter in the hope that you will eventually develop your own.

Even in the relatively simple matter of purchasing prepared glazes there are several things to consider. Glazes are usually classified according to color, type (glossy, transparent or opaque, matte, etc.) and maturing temperature, this designated by cone number. (See Chapter 11 for cone-temperature relationship.) Glaze maturing temperature should be the same as that of the clay it is to be used on. Potters say that glaze must "fit" the body —one which does not fit will show defects in the form of crazing or shivering. Ceramic

dealers sell clays and glazes compounded to be successfully used together—ask your dealer if the clay you are using can be glazed with the glazes you intend to buy.

Buy only those glazes which will mature in temperatures possible to the kiln in which your glazed wares will be fired.

MIXING AND APPLYING GLAZE

If you have purchased powdered glazes, you must first mix these with water of an amount sufficient to make a mixture about as thick as whipping cream. Glazes sold in jars containing the proper amount of water need only be well stirred.

Glaze can be applied to ware in several ways. The common methods are brushing, pouring, dipping and spraying. A soft varnish brush about 1″ wide is needed for brushing glaze. Interiors of bowls, etc., are often glazed by putting glaze in the piece, turning and rolling it until the inside is covered, then pouring off any excess glaze. The outside can be glazed by pouring as well. Place the piece on a screen or sticks placed across the top of a pan and pour glaze over it.

Dipping requires a larger amount of glaze than pouring or brushing—enough to allow complete immersion of the piece—and a vessel large enough to hold the glaze. Piece is merely submerged in the glaze for a few seconds, then removed.

Glaze is usually thinned for spraying. This can be done in a household spray such as those used for insecticides, etc., but an electric gun and compressor made for glaze spraying will do an easier and better job. Place the piece to be sprayed on a bench whirler, turning it so all parts of the piece receive an equal amount of glaze.

All of these methods have advantages and disadvantages. Pouring and brushing require the least equipment and will therefore serve the beginner the best. He should also apply glaze to only those pieces which have been biscuit-fired. Commercial potteries often glaze greenware and bring both clay and glaze to maturity in a single fire but such a practice is highly inadvisable in schools, studios or by the beginner working at home.

To glaze a biscuit-fired piece with brush and pouring methods, first thoroughly sponge it with a clean wet sponge to remove dust and to partially fill the pores of the clay with water. This sponging will reduce the tendency for brush and glaze to stick and overload the surface in spots.

Glaze both sides of flat bowls or plates and outside walls of upright forms by brushing glaze on with short, patting strokes. Some unevenness is inevitable, but since melting and flowing of the glaze will level it more or less, it is not particularly harmful. You will need to apply two, or possibly three, coats before reaching a total thickness of approximately $\frac{1}{16}''$. Cover inside of piece first, either by brushing or pouring. Pour glaze into the form, tip over a pan to swirl and revolve it as you pour glaze out. Do this quickly or an overly thick coat, which may crack before firing or crawl during firing, will be taken up by the damp wall. A too-thick coat may also run down the sides of the piece to form a pool in the bottom which might possibly break the piece as it cools after firing.

Since glaze does run when fired (some more than others, due to composition), give rim edges an extra coat. When glaze has dried so it is no longer sticky, scrape and sponge glaze from bottom surface of the foot and about $\frac{1}{16}''$ of it from the outside bottom edge of the wall. These precautions are taken to prevent glaze from running down and sticking to the kiln shelf.

Permit the glazed piece to dry thoroughly and it is ready for glost-firing.

PARTIAL GLAZE

When a colored body is used, interesting decorative effects may result from glazed and unglazed areas on the same piece. Regardless of the treatment of the outside, the inside surface should be completely glazed if the piece is to be used as a container. To have glazed and unglazed areas on a piece, use wax

Under-glaze colors form design on this bowl.

Apply white matt, partial quick dip in dark gloss for pleasing contrast.

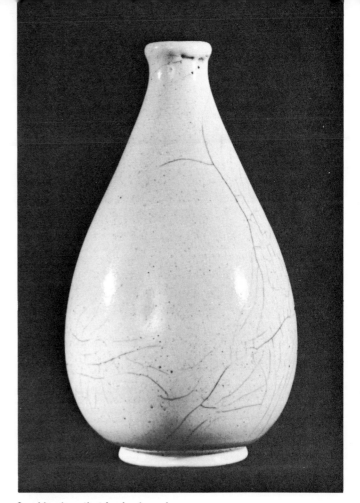

Crackle glaze that is simple and in a pattern adapted to form.

emulsion from a ceramic supply house or make your own from ½ paraffin and ½ kerosene heated over a hot plate until the paraffin has melted, then paint areas with the mixture where you want no glaze. Be sure glaze is not too thick, then apply by brushing, pouring, dipping, or spraying after waxed areas have dried. The wax will resist the glaze coat and when fired will provide contrasting texture of glazed and unglazed areas.

POURING

Decorative effects resulting from pouring glaze may be many and varied. Some glazes work better for pouring than others, owing to their composition. However, most glazes can be used satisfactorily after a little practice. To glaze a pot by pouring, place two 1" square, well-sanded hardwood boards across a large pan. Wax foot of piece and about ½" of wall above foot, then sponge piece with clean damp sponge. Glaze piece inside, then invert on boards over center of pan and use an enameled metal pitcher to pour glaze over outside surface of piece. Move pitcher around as you pour. As soon as glaze surface no longer glistens, pour second coat if desired.

Wax emulsion painted on dark body, white matt brushed over for glazed and unglazed areas.

CLAUDE HORAN

As soon as piece can be handled without glaze sticking to fingers, pour contrasting colored glaze over surface in desired pattern.

DIPPING

To dip-glaze a pot with a smooth uniform coating requires enough glaze and a large enough container that the piece can be completely submerged in a single dipping. Only small pieces should be dip-glazed. Wax the foot and about ½" up the wall from the foot. Permit wax to dry, pour glaze inside small-necked forms, sponge outside with damp sponge, and cover top with a flat circular piece of rigid sheet metal the same size or slightly larger than outside diameter of top rim of the pot. Hold metal disc in place with the thumb, with fingers on foot rim, and submerge in glaze. Set aside and touch up any bare spots on rim with a finger dipped into the glaze.

Open forms are usually dipped without metal disc on rim, glazing both inside and outside at the same time. A quick dip of part of the form in a different colored glaze should be done while the first coat is still damp. A wax pattern may be painted on the first glaze coat and the piece completely or partly dipped in a different-colored glaze before the first coat dries. If the first coat has dried completely, the glaze may crack and peel off or crawl when fired.

CRACKLE GLAZE

A crackle glaze may be desired for its decorative effect on certain pieces. Crackle of a glaze is commonly considered as controlled crazing, which means that it is intentional, not an accident, and has a crackle pattern the potter feels is attractive on the piece. Crazing is caused by unequal thermal expansion and contraction between the body and the glaze. For most potters, to develop a glaze that will not craze is sufficient of a challenge to cause them to use crackle glazes sparingly. There are, however, pieces on which a crackle glaze can be a very desirable decorative feature. Crackle glazes should not be used on containers for liquids, unless the clay body is sufficiently vitrified to prevent sweating which can ruin varnished surfaces.

Assuming we have a glaze which does not craze and we want to make it into a crackle glaze, there are some simple procedures we might follow. First, we can use a clay body which will be underfired (soft and porous) at the temperature at which the glaze matures. Second, if we are mixing our own glaze, we can leave out some of the clay that is part of the glaze composition. Third, we can add calcium phosphate (bone ash) to the glaze. Any of these procedures should cause the glaze to crackle during or soon after firing. Rub India ink over the surface of fired glaze to stain crackle.

GLAZE FAULTS AND DEFECTS

Crazing may prove an actual defect to a glaze. The hundreds of tiny cracks all over the surface of the glaze, which define this fault, may appear during firing or as the piece cools. While crackled glazes are used for certain effects (see earlier), unintended crackling can actually prove harmful to the piece.

GARY OBERBILLIG, GARY PETERS, MARYANN GRAVITT

Pour one colored glaze over another for an interesting pattern.

Crackle glaze lines bowl
banded with matte glaze.

Crazing may be the result of a too-thick application of glaze, or fit of glaze to clay body may be imperfect.

Another common fault is known as crawling. The glaze has gathered in bunches or raised sections and left others bare. This is commonly due to dust or grease on the biscuit ware, or, again, an overly generous application of glaze. To correct, avoid handling biscuit ware—oil from the hands can cause crawling. Sponge piece to remove dust and strive for a coating of glaze about $\frac{1}{16}''$ thick.

Pinholes or small circular pits in the glaze are usually caused by gas bubbles resulting from the burning of carbonaceous materials from the glaze. The fault can be corrected by firing more slowly or to a higher temperature. Pinholing is also caused when sandpaper is used to smooth clay. Sandpaper is not a ceramic tool and sanding of ceramic surfaces is not a desirable practice. It can be a ruinous one when pieces are to be subsequently glazed as the flints and various natural and synthetic minerals used to coat sandpaper are often incompatible with glaze ingredients—bits of these ground into a clay surface cause defects in the glaze surface.

Devitrification is recognized by a rough scum on the glaze surface. It is caused by too much silica in the glaze and may be corrected by an addition of china clay. A rough and sandy glaze may be the result of a too-thin glaze application, insufficient firing, or some glaze ingredient may have needed more grinding.

Sulfuring may result from sulfur in the fuel used to fire the kiln, the water, some coloring oxides or other glaze ingredients. Result may be a blistered, dry or shriveled glaze. Blisters are also sometimes the result of too short a firing period or the presence of smoke in the kiln. Check for cracks in the muffle, if smoke is suspected; try distilled water or change of glaze ingredients if sulfur seems the cause of the trouble.

GLAZE-MAKING EXPERIMENTS

Here is a relatively simple method of experimenting with glaze compositions. It requires no knowledge of chemistry and only the most elementary knowledge of arithmetic. You will need a balance scale which weighs in grams, a 60-mesh screen, a small mortar and pestle, three or four water color brushes, a 1″ varnish brush and a ceramic marking pencil in black.

The first ingredient you will need is a commercial glaze frit. Frit is a carefully calculated and compounded glass which has been fused and powdered. Frits, identified by number, are sold at ceramic supply houses. Choose one with a maturing point within the firing range of the kiln available. There are many glaze frits, each with a different chemical composition. Any of the following will produce interesting results: #71—contains lead, sodium, alumina and silica; #24—contains lead, sodium, potassium, calcium, alumina, boron, silica and zirconium; #3304—contains lead, sodium, alumina and silica; #3110—contains potassium, sodium, calcium, magnesium, alumina, boron and silica. Purchase an amount of one of these and some bentonite.

TEST TILES

Make twenty-five or fifty test tiles by rolling out clay slab ¼″ thick and cutting it into strips 1¼″ wide and 3″ long. Bend strips to form L's. Punch hole ¼″ at center of the upright part of the tile. Biscuit-fire at temperature used for your ware.

Your balance scales should be of the type that has a bar marked in $\frac{1}{10}$ grams and capable of weighing 10 grams. You should also have weights to include one or two 200 grams, one 100 grams, one 50 grams, two 20, two 2, and one each of 10-, 5- and 1-gram weights.

Be sure the scale is balanced. When it is in balance, needle between the pans will remain stationary at center line. Weight on the bar must be at extreme left. Place weights totaling 97 grams in the pan on the right. Place frit on the left pan until the needle stops at center line on indicator. Place weighed frit in mixing bowl. Remove weights from pan and move weight on the bar until the left edge of it is in line with the #3 on bar. Place powdered bentonite in the left pan until needle again indicates a balance. Add weighed bentonite to frit and stir together.

Then bentonite and frit will form the basic glaze composition. Use the varnish brush to work it through screen twice—if there is a residue left in the screen, grind it in mortar with pestle until it will pass through the mesh. Put these combined ingredients in a covered jar and identify it with a label stating the number of the frit used; that mix contains 97 percent frit plus 3 percent bentonite: total 100 percent.

To make a test of the base mixture for firing, weigh out 10 grams of it and place it in the mortar. Adding one drop of water at a time, grind with pestle until mixture is of the consistency of medium-weight whipping cream. Brush on inside surfaces of a test tile. Use the black marking pencil and label the tile on the back to indicate glaze composition as you did on the jar label. Fire the test.

ANALYZING TEST RESULTS

Examine the fired test tile and consider how it might be improved; what changes you would like to make in it. Additions of various glaze materials in weighed percentages will improve glaze fit if crazing is present, will make glaze more, or less, fluid, will vary glaze texture, make it opaque and add color to it. The effects of some of the materials commonly used to influence such matters are given in the following paragraphs.

Additions of powdered white lead, red lead, litharge, borax and soda ash in amounts of 5 to 15 percent will lower the melting point and increase fluidity.

The addition of rutile and titanium dioxide in amounts of 5 to 15 percent produce a matte texture and may make glaze cream or buff colored.

Additions of ball clay, china clay or kaolin in amounts of 5 to 25 percent will raise melting point of glaze, may help crazing, and in larger percentages produce matte texture.

Additions of tin oxide, Zircopax, Ultrox and such opacifying compounds may raise the fusion point of the glaze and help in correcting crazing. Usually 5 to 10 percent is sufficient to make glaze opaque or white.

Additions of feldspar or whiting in amounts of 5 to 25 percent will increase viscosity, may help glaze fit, raise fusion point and tend to develop matte texture.

Flint increases viscosity, raises fusion point and may cause or correct crazing. Add in amounts of 10 to 20 percent.

For purposes of illustration, we will assume that the first test tile of the base glaze was satisfactory in gloss, but glaze was slightly too fluid and had crazed somewhat. Record these observations in a notebook set aside for the purpose. Give the test tile a number and transfer this number to noted observations regarding the tile. Keep tile also.

The next step in the glaze experiment is to correct faults of crazing and over-fluidity in the base glaze. A study of the above materials and their effects will help you select one to improve the base glaze. Again, for illustrative purposes, we will use china clay.

Throughout this series of experiments all materials will be added as plus percentages to the original 100 percent total of frit and bentonite. We now propose to add 5 percent to the original 100. To do this, weigh out 10 grams of base mixture and place in mortar. Weigh ½ gram china clay. Remember that .1 of a gram equals 1 percent of ten grams, .5 gram (½ gram) equals 5 percent of 10 grams, so we are adding 5 percent of china clay to our original mixture as a plus addition.

Glazes are of many types, glossy or dull.

Grind new mixture in mortar with water as before, apply to test tile, label back of tile and fire. Make additional tests using 10, 15, 20, and 25 percent additions of china clay. Fire and record results.

We will assume that the tile with the addition of 15 percent of china clay has a glaze no longer too fluid or crazed. If this series had not solved the problem, another material would have been chosen and the work repeated.

Adjust the remaining basic mixture by adding 15 percent china clay to it. This is accomplished by first weighing the remainder. There should be 50 grams left; add 7.5 grams china clay and screen combined materials twice as described before.

To make tests to produce an opaque glaze, weigh adjusted base mixture into five equal parts of 11.5 grams. To the first part add .2 gram tin oxide. To the second part add .4 gram, to the third .6 gram, to the fourth .8 gram and to the fifth, 1 gram of tin oxide. Prepare tiles, fire, make records and observations, and select the best, as before.

MIXING GLAZES. 1. Weigh ingredients on scale.

2. Add water to glaze in mortar and pestle.

3. Apply glaze to test tiles and label tiles.

To carry on with the example, we will assume that the 8 percent addition gave the most satisfactory results. This would make the glaze composition as follows: frit, 97 grams; bentonite, 3 grams; china clay, 15 grams, and tin, 8 grams. Mix several hundred grams of glaze, screen it thoroughly, and you are ready to make experiments for color.

Using the metallic oxides listed in the accompanying table, run a complete series of experiments for color. Use the basic unit of 10 grams, adding certain percentages as plus figures. Remember that .1 of a gram is 1 per cent of 10 grams.

Colors will be influenced by quantities of colorant used, by kiln temperature, by the basic frit ingredients and by kiln atmosphere.

Some oxides have been combined with others or calcined alone; they often offer interesting variations. Examples are potassium dichromate, iron chromate, red lead chromate, and burnt sienna and burnt umber. For most of the maroons, crimsons, and pinks, a frit containing calcium should be used with tin oxide and a commercial maroon, crimson, or pink glaze stain (prepared glazed pigments). For good strong yellows, use commercial stains with a frit containing no calcium; an addition of tin should be desirable here.

You may find your glazes to be speckled. The speckles are concentrations of color caused by insufficient grinding. Many feel that these are desirable but if you find lack of uniformity in color objectionable, talk to your supply dealer about acquiring a ball mill.

On the next pages are given a number of base glazes which fire at different cones, for which materials are presented in parts by weight, along with a table of ingredients for making colored slips and also for adding color to the base glazes.

SOURCES FOR FRITS AND GLAZE MATERIALS

L. H. Butcher Co.
  15th & Vermont Streets, San Francisco, Calif.
  3628 East Olympic Blvd., Los Angeles, Calif.
  1703 Sixth Avenue, South, Seattle, Washington
  15th & N.W. Johnson Streets, Portland, Oregon
  520 W. Second South Street, Salt Lake City, Utah
Allied Engineering Division of Ferro Corp.
  4150 East 56th Street, Cleveland, Ohio
  Western Agency: Western Ceramic Supply Co., 1601
    Howard Street, San Francisco, Calif.
B. F. Drakenfield & Co., Inc.
  45-47 Park Place, New York City, New York
Mason Color & Chemical Works, Inc.
  East Liverpool, Ohio
Ceramic Color & Chemical Co.
  New Brighton, Penna.
Pemco Division of the Glidden Co.
  5601 Eastern Ave., Baltimore, Maryland
Moore and Munger
  33 Rector Street, New York City, New York

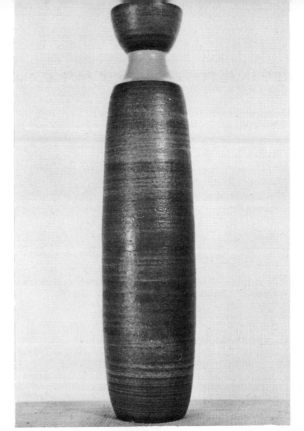

Tall, symmetrical bottle with
brown and tan matt glaze

TABLE FOR MIXING DECORATIVE SLIPS

To 100 grams of white firing pottery and modeling clay

ADD:	TO MAKE:
4 grams iron chromate	Gray
4 grams Mason Brown Stain #204	Brown
10 grams red iron oxide	Red-brown
4 grams Mason Blue-Green Stain #7	Blue-green
1 to 4 grams chromium oxide	Green
15 grams Mason Pink Underglaze #163	Pink
5 grams Blue Stain	Blue
4 grams cobalt oxide	Dark blue
5 grams Ceramic Color & Chem. Co. Yellow Stain #1335	Yellow
6 to 8 grams Black Stain	Black

To prepare for use: Mix and grind ingredients in mortar and put through 80-mesh screen. Add water to make thick cream consistency—thin for spraying.

Stoneware bottle with finger-painted
decoration, high glaze.

CHART OF % OF OXIDE ADDITIONS TO FRITS OR BASE GLAZES SHOWN

Antimony oxide	2%
Cobalt oxide	1%
Copper oxide	2%
Chromium oxide	1%
Crocus martis	4%
Molybdenum oxide	2%
Manganese oxide	2%
Nickel oxide	2%
Red iron oxide	4–8%
Rutile	5–10%
Tin oxide	5–10%
Vanadium oxide	2%

Note: A larger percentage will darken the color; less will make it lighter.

GLAZE I. Cone 06-04. Orange (gloss red specks). Trent Thompson

White lead	42.4
Soda ash	7.4
Lithium carbonate	5.1
Potassium carbonate	3.5
Whiting	1.9
Kaolin	13.4
Flints	26.3
	100.0
Chromium oxide	.25
Molybdenum oxide	1.50

Note: Better specks when sprayed.

GLAZE II. Cone 06-04. Textured gloss. Bob Noll

Plastic vitrox (PV clay)	50
Colemanite	50
	100.00

Add to 100.00%:

Red iron oxide	4.
Manganese carbonate	1.
Rutile	7.
Vanadium oxide	10.

GLAZE III. Cone 05. Imitation stoneware. Bob Noll

Del Monte spar	28.2
Nephelene syenite	21.2
Borax	1.3
Colemanite	6.0
Fluorspar	11.2

Lithium carbonate	5.8
Zinc oxide	2.7
Flint	11.3
Strontium carbonate	11.3
EPK	15.0
	115.0

Add:

Red iron oxide	4.0
Manganese	1.0
	120.0

Note: Rough when thin; velvety when thick.

GLAZE IV. Cone 02. Semi-matt. Nancy Lynch

White lead	31.2
Potassium carbonate	7.1
Whiting	5.4
Zinc oxide	6.1
Clay	25.8
Flint	24.3

Note: May develop pitted texture when heavy.

GLAZE V. Cone 02. Semi-glass. Jan Jones

White lead	34.4
Pearl ash	6.3
Whiting	2.1
Barium carbonate	13.1
China clay	22.7
Flint	21.4

GLAZE VI. Cone 2. Slightly fluid matt. Jan Jones

Nephelene syenite	46.65
Whiting	18.15
Zinc oxide	14.89
Magnesium carbonate	.16
Clay	1.33
Flint	19.02

GLAZE VII. Cone 2. Waxy matt. Nancy Lynch

Nephelene syenite	44.9
Magnesium carbonate	4.0
Zinc oxide	2.9
White lead	25.1
Clay	22.3
Flint	.8

GLAZE VIII. Cone 2.
Gloss. Robert Smith

Kona A-3 feldspar	66.80
Soda ash	.16
Whiting	4.46
Zinc oxide	2.23
White lead	26.32

GLAZE IX. Cone 5-6. Leadless
barium matt. Warren Westerberg

Del Monte feldspar	60.9
Whiting	13.2
Barium carbonate	25.9

Note: Good in either oxidation or reduction. Very good for colors.

GLAZE X. Cone 5. Fluid leadless
opalescent glaze. Mary Auvil

Frit #3110	52.32
Colemanite	13.38
Whiting	.05
Lithium carbonate	1.31
Strontium carbonate	10.50
Kaolin	10.69
Flint	11.75
Rutile	4% addition

Note: Excellent with coloring oxides. Do not apply too heavily. Good in oxidation or reduction fire. Best over dark body; also fires good glossy coat at cone 2.

GLAZE XI. Cone 5-6. Waxy
semi-gloss. Joan Bugbee

Del Monte spar	89.04
Whiting	2.76
Barium carbonate	5.47
White lead	2.73

Note: For excellent opaque semi-gloss add 8% tin plus coloring oxides. For waxy matt add 10% rutile and coloring oxides.

GLAZE XII. Cone 5. Dead stony
matt. Fred Lucero

Kona K4 feldspar	113.4
Zinc oxide	19.2
Barium carbonate	35.1
Clay	18.6
Flint	11.8
Rutile	1.9

GLAZE XIII. Cone 5. Textured mottled
semi-gloss glaze. Trent Thompson

Kona F4 feldspar	37.79
Whiting	9.82
White lead	21.87
Lithium carbonate	1.05
Kaolin	14.20
Flint	15.27
	100.00
Vanadium oxide	2% addition

Note: Grind glaze, add vanadium and stir in, then apply with a brush. Good in oxidation or reduction. Eggshell in oxidation, darker in reduction.

GLAZE XIV. Cone 5. Cecile McCann

Nephelene syenite	55.73
Barium carbonate	15.83
White lead	12.94
Lithium carbonate	2.47
Boric acid	1.56
Kaolin	1.73
Flint	9.76

Note: Good in oxidation firing. In reduction, with addition of 1.5% copper oxide, .25% Cr_2O_3, will give reds where thin, greens where thick; CuO plus $CoCO_3$ give red and blue. If mixed and used immediately, glaze has a very smooth texture. If used after standing for several days, glaze will give a bubbled, blistered surface.

GLAZE XV. Cone 7. Gloss glaze.
Robert Smith

Nephelene syenite	63.80
Dolomite	8.47
Whiting	4.61
Zinc oxide	11.20
White lead	11.88

Add 5% tin oxide and coloring oxides.

GLAZE XVI. Cone 7. Dry matt.
Joan Bugbee

Nephelene syenite	56.34
Barium carbonate	24.02
Whiting	19.61

Note: Lithium carbonate, soda ash, and potassium carbonate are soluble in water, so glazes containing these materials should be stored dry and when mixed with water used immediately.

Matching pitchers made
on the wheel. Clay is stoneware,
glaze seaweed ash.

9 · Wheel-Built Forms

It is not known when, or where, clay ware was first formed on the potter's wheel. Credit for the invention of the wheel has been given to most of the great cultures of the past—very early Chinese pottery pieces show marks indicating use of the wheel; paintings on Egyptian tombs and on Greek vases show wheels used for pottery making—but it may or may not have been an independent discovery in each country.

It is known that the potter's wheel has undergone many changes in form. The wheel shown in Egyptian tomb engravings and on Greek pottery was mounted on a pedestal and turned by hand. The Chinese and Japanese still use a wheel mounted at approximately floor level. The wheel head is a large and heavy circular disk. There are holes around its periphery and the potter, squatted or seated cross-legged before it, inserts a stick in one of the holes and turns the wheel in a counterclockwise direction until it is revolving rapidly.

A type of wheel commonly adapted for studio use today is the kick wheel with head fastened to an upright shaft over a heavy flywheel. The shaft is attached at the bottom to a horizontally moving treadle. The potter stands before the wheel on his right foot and turns the wheel by pressing and releasing the treadle with the left. Another wheel which is foot-operated is commonly known as the European kick wheel. In this, the wheel head is set at the top of the upright shaft. A large and heavy flywheel or circular disk is mounted on the bottom of the shaft to turn on a horizontal plane. The potter is seated on a bench built as part of the wheel and operates it by kicking the lower disk with the ball of his right foot, setting both upper and lower disks to turning in a counterclockwise direction.

Kick wheels allow the potter to speed or slow the wheel at will as the work demands. The electrically powered wheels commercially available usually operate at constant speeds which are changed by changing belts. One expensive type permits variable speeds through inclusion of a controlling rheostat.

If you have a knack for carpentry and a measure of ingenuity, you can readily build a wheel of your own. Some dealers sell kits that contain the wheelhead, shaft, bearings, and flywheel. Or you can improvise the wheel assembly from used automobile parts, bought at a wrecking yard. The wheel should be mounted absolutely level in a sturdy housing. A successful home-built wheel is shown in Chapter 12.

The steps in making pottery forms on a wheel are known as throwing and are the same regardless of type of wheel used. Mastery of the wheel may take considerable practice but it provides the same challenge to the craftsman as those presented by the important phases of any worthwhile craft. Keep in mind that today's master potters were also once beginners.

CLAY FOR THROWING

The clay you will use for throwing may be the same as that used for other methods of building. Pottery clays with a small addition of fine grog or those without added grog may be used. Thorough wedging of clay is important in this method. It should be moderately stiff, be completely uniform in texture and be free of lumps or air bubbles. Lumps, hard or soft, or incorporated air bubbles will distort the form being thrown.

TOOLS FOR THROWING

The first of these is a suitable wheel. Others are a sharp ice pick or awl for trimming cylinder rims, a length of piano or other strong, fine wire for cutting forms loose from bats or wheel head, and a trimming tool for turning excess clay from form bottoms, etc.

Accessory needs are plaster bats or aluminum plates to set over wheel head when throwing, a pan or bowl to hold water close to the work for lubricating hands and clay while throwing, and sponges for lubricating, smoothing and clean-up operations. One sponge should be a small "elephant-ear," the best shape for smoothing finished ware.

DENNIS HERRING

Wheel-thrown bowl
with flanged lid.

THROWING

A thrown piece of pottery is formed by the potter's hands as the clay revolves as an integral part of the wheel head. The head is usually a metal disk which revolves on a horizontal plane—as truly horizontal as possible or true verticals will not be achieved in throwing. The metal disk may be aluminum, brass, iron or steel; preferably a non-rusting material. Some potters prefer to do the throwing directly on this metal disk; others cover it with aluminum plates which have holes placed to fit over set-screws in the wheel head, or simply fasten plaster bats to the wheel head with clay slip. Added bats or plates have an advantage in that they can be removed without cutting the thrown piece loose at the bottom and this makes it easier to recenter piece for trimming. The beginner is advised to use removable bats or plates.

STEPS IN THE THROWING PROCESS

Start by wedging a mass of clay about the size of an indoor baseball, or a little larger, and pat and smack it into a round, smooth ball. Slap ball lightly on center of wheel, using sufficient force to flatten it slightly on the bottom. Metal heads should be dry when clay is put on them for throwing or clay will slip and slide instead of turning as an integral part of the wheel— as it must do. A plaster bat should be moist when clay is put on it or clay may come loose from the bottom when the piece is only partly formed. Help clay cling to either plaster or metal surface by first patting ball all around sides, pressing down toward the wheel head, until you have a cone-shaped mound. This will also prevent water from getting between clay and metal plate.

CENTERING

The first step in throwing is centering the ball of clay on the wheel head. Start wheel turning counterclockwise. When it is turning quite rapidly, dip hands in water and clasp the clay mound in both hands. Exert uniform pressure

82

BOWL. 1. Sprinkle ball of clay to lubricate.

4. Exert uniform pressure from all sides.

7. Keep fingers stiff, bend wrists outward.

2. Under pressure, clay rises to make cone.

3. Flatten cone with downward pressure.

5. Make well by pressing left thumb in mound.

6. Remove excess water from well with sponge.

8. Flare bowl sides with gradual pressure.

9. Note how wall is spread between hands.

CYLINDRICAL FORM. 1. Start by making well.

2. Left-hand fingers press wall on inside.

3. Right-hand knuckle presses against outside.

4. Bring hands slowly upward to pull up wall.

5. If wall spreads, collar it in both hands.

6. Leave wall slightly thicker at bottom.

from all sides until clay spins smoothly and shows no irregular motion as the wheel revolves. Lubricate the clay and hands as often as needed, for if the clay drags under the hands, centering it will be impossible. If the left elbow is braced firmly against the body and the left forearm held rigid as the lower part of the palm of the left hand is pressed against the clay, combined weight of body, arm and hand will force revolving clay to wheel center. Use the right hand to sprinkle water on the clay and to pull it toward you as the left is pressing it away from you.

Under this pressure, clay will rise in a cone. Some potters spin clay into a cone, then press it down by flattening it with the thumbs several times before forming the low flattened mound which is the starting shape for forming the cylinder.

The cylinder is the basic shape from which all other thrown forms are developed. It will be worthwhile to practice making cylinders before attempting other forms.

MAKING THE WELL

This is the next step after the ball is centered and shaped into a low flattened mound. Support mound with the right hand and clamp fingers of the left over the right with the left thumb tip resting on the center of the clay mound. Insert the left thumb into the mound, leaving enough clay between thumb and wheel head to form the bottom of the piece.

SPREADING THE BALL

When the well is made, you are ready to spread the ball. This is done with hands held in the same position as for making the well but with the left thumb brought toward the supporting hand to cause the clay to flow and expand ahead of the thumb. When the ball is spread to make an opening of the desired diameter for the inside bottom of the piece, you are ready to pull up the walls of the cylinder.

PULLING UP THE CYLINDER

When clay ball is spread to form inside bottom of piece, lubricate hands and clay and place the left hand inside opening with fingers extended and cupped slightly. Permit finger ends to rest on the inside bottom with pads against the wall. Double right hand to make a loose fist—notice cushion thus formed by side of first finger at second joint. It is this cushion which does the work on the outside of the cylinder. Rest the knuckles of your right-hand fist against the wheel head at bottom of the clay and start the wheel. Exert pressure uniformly with both right and left hands. As soon as the clay forms a slight bulge above fingers, you have pressed hard enough. Without increasing pressure, bring hands slowly upwards, pulling or pushing clay bulge ahead of them.

To help in keeping pressure uniform and unwavering, think of your arms and shoulders as forming a C-clamp. "Set" this C-clamp and then draw up hands to form wall. Do not stop the pulling-up process in the middle of the cylinder wall at any time or the finished piece will have irregularities in wall thickness. Start at the base, holding hands in set position, and draw them up and above clay; then release. Repeat to make walls higher and thinner until all the clay from the ball has been drawn into the cylinder.

Cylinder should be straight and vertical. You may find that the form tends to spread at the

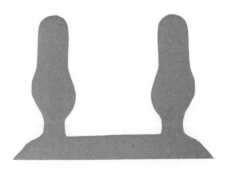

When clay forms slight bulge, draw up.

85

Think of arms and
shoulders as a C-clamp.

top. Control this by contracting cylinder top after each pulling-up by circling outside of the piece with both hands and pressing wall inward. Wall of the completed cylinder should be slightly thicker at the base than at top. If wall is higher on one side of the piece than the other, or if one side of it is thicker than the other, it means that clay was not perfectly centered at the start of the throwing. Slight unevenness in rim can be trimmed away with the ice pick or similar tool. To trim, support the clay edge between the first finger and thumb of the left hand and brace the end of the ice pick against right thumb with point about $\frac{1}{4}''$ from the top of the cylinder wall. As the wheel revolves, press point of pick through clay to cut it off.

SHAPING THE CYLINDER

There are a few standard operations which apply in the development of any wheel-made form from the thrown cylinder. Wheel speed is rather slow and hands are comparatively dry though lubricated. Left hand should be inside cylinder with finger ends directly opposite those of the right hand which is on the outside of the pot. Pressure from inside fingers expands the form while those on the outside restrain it. Pressure from outside will cause form to contract at point of pressure. It is usually best to draw form in by applying uniform opposing pressures with the fingers of both hands.

Do not attempt to develop the form in one operation, but repeat process several times. After each operation, study the developing form and work in desired refinements in contour in successive operations.

To finish the form, smooth and burnish the outside by holding the ball of the first finger of the right hand against the revolving shape. Inside support is furnished throughout the finishing by finger ends of the left hand.

If piece sags, lacks symmetry or looks unpleasantly heavy, clay may have become too wet during throwing, wall is of uneven thickness or was made too thin.

MAKING A BOWL

To make a bowl from the cylinder, first decide on the approximate shape. A flaring bowl is formed by extending the fingers of both hands and using entire surface of hands and fingers to form the bowl. Keep fingers stiff and close together. Place left hand inside cylinder with fingers resting on the bottom and palm side of hand against wall. The right hand is placed directly opposite on outside of wall. Bend the wrist to spread the cylinder at the top, pressing the clay wall to form from the inside. The outside hand acts as control and guard.

OVOID AND SPHEROID FORMS

To make the ovoid (egg-shaped) or the spheroid (round) form, use left hand, slightly cupped and with finger pads against base of inner wall to oppose those of the right hand on the outside. Apply medium pressure at the base of the wall, increasing it as you approach the central area to cause the wall to expand. As hands near the top, pressure is gradually decreased from the inside and increased from the outside. Repeat forming process several times until desired results are achieved.

Bowls in these forms would be developed in the same way; pressure applied where needed to expand or contract the form outline. Plate forms are developed from low cylinders, pro-

FINISHING. 1. To trim bottom, invert on wheel.

2. Center and anchor in place with coil.

3. Use trimming tool to cut away excess clay.

4. Recess bottom of piece to make foot rim.

5. Shave lightly to refine outlines of shape.

6. Sponge to remove cutting tool marks.

PITCHER. 1. First step: pull up cylinder.

2. Round form with pressure from inside.

3. Draw top in with pressure from outside.

4. Trim and round top edge, flare slightly.

5. Sponge and smooth completed form.

6. Form lip between thumb and fingers.

cedure much like that of making the flared conical bowl.

When any wheel-made form is complete, sponge edge of rim with wet elephant-ear sponge to smooth and round it slightly and set the piece away to dry to leather-hardness.

To make duplicate forms—a set of cups or plates—the clay should be weighed into duplicate amounts.

THE PULLED SPOUT

If the form you have made suggests a pitcher, pull a spout in the edge rim. Support the rim on the outside with two fingers of the left hand spread apart. With first finger of the right hand, stroke the clay upward and outward on inside of rim between the two spread fingers. A light downward direction at the rim will help to make spout a dripless one.

TRIMMING AND FINISHING

The process of cutting and shaving the outside surface of the leather-hard thrown form to perfect profile irregularities and finish it, is called either turning or trimming. Trimming is a proper part of the throwing process although skilfully thrown pieces will need less cutting and shaving to perfect them and it is the aim of all potters to keep this part of the work at a minimum.

As soon as your thrown pot is leather-hard, return it to the wheel and center it. If loose from bat, fasten it in place with a coil of clay to trim or refine the top area. Use the trimming tool for cutting, then smooth with wet sponge.

In order to trim and turn a foot in the bottom area, cut loose, if necessary, from the wheel head and invert the form. Center it on the wheel head and fasten in place with a coil of clay. Cut the foot rim by recessing the bottom of the piece and do any necessary refining of line in the lower part of the shape. The piece should never be trimmed on the inside.

PULLED HANDLE. 1. Start with tapered clay wad.

2. Wet hand and pull over clay.

3. Stroking and squeezing lengthens clay.

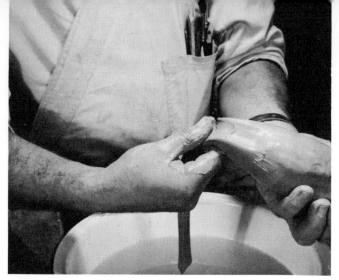

4. Bend the tapered, pulled strip to make handle.

5. Handle may be applied directly to form.

6. The pulled handle has a fluid, plastic quality.

Let wheel revolve rather slowly as the trimming process proceeds. Hold trimming tool at an angle which allows it to cut clean without scraping. When trimming is complete, sponge to smooth cut surfaces and sign your piece on the bottom before you set it away to dry for firing.

THE PULLED HANDLE

This is the ideal handle for the thrown piece because of its plastic, fluid quality. To make a pulled handle, wedge a quantity of stiff but plastic clay and pat it into a tapered wad. Grasp the heaviest end of the wad tightly in the left hand. Wet the right hand with water and pull it over the tapered clay with a gradually tightening squeeze. This downward stroking, squeezing motion, done repeatedly, will cause the clay to lengthen. The shape of the lengthening strip is controlled by the pulling of the right hand and the position of the fingers throughout the operation. The part of the strip used to make the handle will taper; the thicker part forms the top of the handle.

The pulled handle may be applied directly to the form which is leather-hard. If it is too plastic for immediate application, it can be dried somewhat on a plaster bat.

If handle is applied immediately after pulling, the surface of the leather-hard pot is prepared by applying water to a scored surface made where both top and bottom of handle will join to pot and the pot allowed to set for five minutes before handle is applied. If handle has been permitted to harden slightly, heavy slip instead of water should be applied to scored surfaces on the pot.

In planning a handle for any piece, attempt to make it of a size and shape to suit it to the piece for both function and appearance. Imagination must take the place of actual test for function, as obviously the piece cannot be lifted by the handle at this stage. Remember, too, that the space enclosed by the handle is a part of the design and should be carefully

THROWN SPOUT. 1. Form on wheel to plan.

3. Mark position on leather-hard form.

2. When stiffened, cut at desired angle.

4. Pierce strainer holes within outline.

5. Score and paint joints with slip.

6. Seal joints with pressure from tool.

FLANGED LID. 1. First, measure opening.

2. Check measurements with calipers.

3. Fit flange and place lid on form.

4. Center pot, trim curve of lid top.

5. Prepare lid top and knob for joining.

6. Attaching knob completes teapot.

SLAB SPOUT. 1. Plan with paper pattern.

2. Use pattern for cutting clay shape.

3. Position on form and mark.

4. Pierce strainer holes in lower area.

5. Score, add slip to joints, model firmly.

6. Sponge and smooth joint on finished form.

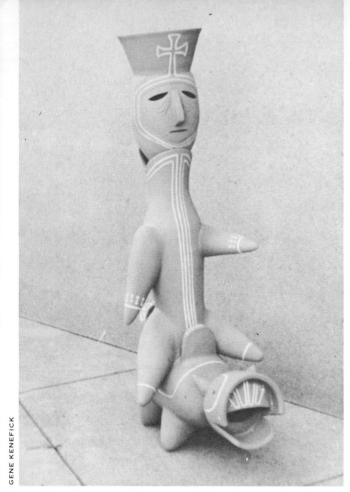

The Crusader, a wheel sculpture

planned as to form and size in relation to the piece upon which it is placed.

LIDS AND SPOUTS

Lids and spouts add to both design and function of the thrown piece. They can be thrown and trimmed on the wheel or formed as slabs. The tea pot illustrated shows the steps in making thrown spout and lid.

WHEEL-MADE SCULPTURE

Nothing will give you more feeling of accomplishment than your first successful thrown sculpture.

In thrown sculpture forms, all unnecessary detail is eliminated and the plastic quality of the forms emphasized. For your first attempts you should make many sketches or drawings

of the sculpture you wish to make. Sketches help to establish dimensions and proportions of the various forms and their relationship in the completed sculpture. Later you may wish to design each form on the wheel as you go, but this procedure requires some background or experience.

Once you have established dimensions and proportions in your thinking, you are ready to throw the various forms. The foundation unit should be thrown first. This provides a basis of comparison for related forms or appendages. Next throw the related forms in scale with the foundation form. All forms to complete the sculpture should be thrown during a single working period and all placed in a closed box or cupboard. As soon as the clay will not stick to your fingers, all necessary trimming should be done and the pieces assembled. In assembling the forms, try and retain a maximum of thrown quality. If possible, avoid cutting the foundation piece since to cut it would decrease its strength. Check all appendages against the foundation form for position and size and cut to fit. Apply appendages by deeply scoring joining surfaces and coating the scored areas with heavy slip. Press the joining surfaces firmly together with a slight rocking motion, increasing pressure until they are solidly joined. Permit resulting ridge or bead of slip pressed out of the joint to remain until leather-hard and clean it carefully away. Avoid carving or scraping thrown form; if flattened areas are desired, press them gently but firmly into shape before joining. If necessary, appendages can be curved or bent after they are in position. If they have become rigid, wrap them with damp cheesecloth until they are sufficiently plastic to bend. Any closed forms should have concealed vent holes to permit enclosed air to escape during drying and firing shrinkage.

The pair of chickens shown here were made by George Eimers and are each composed of a bottle form, closed at the top, and two sections of a conical form. The sections of the cone make the base and tail for each bird. The forms were trimmed and assembled as soon as they had reached the early stages of leather-hardness and could be handled without losing shape. In assembling, the bottle form was tipped at the desired angle and mounted on the narrow section of cone. Both the base and area on the bottle to be joined were scored and coated with slip, then pressed and worked solidly together, after which all edges were welded. The second section of cone was then cut to fit and joined in the same manner. The beak, comb and wattles were the last parts applied. The beaks are solid cones modeled by hand, and the combs and wattles are made from slabs of clay, all applied in the same manner. The clay used was an especially compounded body containing 10 percent manganese dioxide. The result is a grayed purpled-brown matte surface, unglazed.

The Crusader made by Gene Kenefick is considerably more complicated. The horse's body and head are one piece composed of a slightly ovoid cylinder which has been contracted to form a neck and flared at the top to form the mouth. The body of the Crusader figure is a similar form with the desired curvature in the torso. The Crusader's head is an ovoid bottle form inverted, the bottle neck fastened into position inside the open top of the torso. The crown is a truncated cone form cut to fit the head, the arms and legs are long tapering cones, while the animal legs and tail are short stubby cones. The saddle and the horse's teeth are slabs cut to fit. All parts were fitted and assembled when they were leather-hard, the joining surfaces having been deeply scored, moistened with water, then coated with heavy slip. In the late stages of leather-hardness, the whole sculpture was coated with a black slip and the details and highlights worked out in sgraffito. In assembling the Crusader, the horse's legs were applied, then the torso was fastened in position; next the arms, legs, sad-dle and horse's teeth and tail were assembled, and last of all the head and crown were fastened in place.

The steps in making the Bull are shown in the accompanying photographs.

In making sculptures on the wheel, always retain the thrown quality of the forms in the finished product. This does not mean that forms cannot be flattened or pressed into variations of the original thrown shape if desirable or necessary. It does mean, however, that carving or elaborate modeling of the forms only detracts from their appeal as thrown sculpture and would be more honest if done by some other process more in keeping with the result.

J. GEORGE EIMERS

Hen and Rooster, wheel sculptures

95

WHEEL SCULPTURE. 1. Thrown parts needed for Bull.

2. Apply slip to scored areas.

3. Press neck firmly into place, then weld.

4. Place head in position.

5. Leg ready for assembly. Note vent holes.

6. Sgraffito pattern on coating of black slip.

COIL-AND-THROW PROCESS

The coil-and-throw process is an ancient Korean technique still used by some potters of Japan. To make a large bowl, pat out a pancake of clay on wheel. Turn wheel and use needle to cut diameter. Use coils 1″ in diameter to build 3″ to 5″ of cylinder. With damp hands, smooth coils as wheel turns. Let set for an hour or two, add four or five more coils, smooth, and let set again. When cylinder is 2/3 final height, expand form to 1/3 finished size. Add the final coils and finish shaping. (Demonstration by Joe Hysong.)

COIL AND THROW. 1. One-inch coils build cylinder.

2. Smooth coils with damp hands as wheel turns.

3. After hardening, add 4 or 5 more coils.

4. When ⅔ final, expand to ⅓ finished size.

5. When all coils added, throw to final shape.

THROWING FROM A MOUND

Throwing from the top of a mound saves time when making small pieces. Warren Westerberg demonstrates the process. Roughly center large quantity of clay in cone-shaped mound. At top, center amount required for form. With thumb and first finger of left hand make groove below centered top. Support centered portion with hands as both thumbs make well and spread the ball. Pull up cylinder and shape. Cut piece loose from mound with nylon thread.

MOUND THROWING. 1. Center top of mound.

2. Support clay as thumbs make well, spread ball.

3. Pull up the wall.

4. Cut form from mound with nylon thread.

5. Lift from mound with both hands.

THROWING LARGE FORMS

Sometimes the clay required to throw a large piece is more than you or the wheel can handle. To make large forms, throw several sections one at a time and assemble them as shown in the series below, or coil and throw form. Either method takes practice.

SECTIONAL FORMS

To make a sectional form you need a pair of calipers, since joining sections must have the same diameter and wall thickness. The first section is a cylinder with a bottom; the other sections are thrown without bottoms. Throw all sections and carefully check joining di-

SECTIONAL FORM. 1. Score joining surfaces and coat with thick slip.

2. Invert the second section and press it firmly into position.

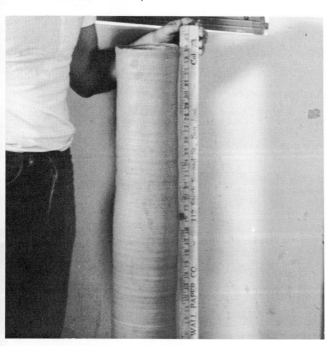

3. Cut plate loose with wire, add third section. Three sections assembled are 34″ high.

4. Throw neck from thick wall at the top of the cylinder.

ameters with calipers. Set sections aside as you finish, and let them sit until they have hardened enough to support each other. This should be at early stage of leather hardness. Deeply score joining surfaces and join together with thick slip. Press sections firmly together and weld joints inside and outside. Joints may be paddled with a downward dragging motion of the paddle from one section to another while one hand supports wall inside. Leave the last section with thick wall at the wheel head, then when inverted in assembly moisten the thick wall and throw neck. When leather hard, trim any irregularities, cut the form from wheel, and bump bottom concave. (Demonstration by Jan Jones.)

NON-SYMMETRICAL FORMS

Develop pleasing variations in symmetry by pressing with the hands, by paddling, or by fluting with the fingers immediately after throwing or when form is leather hard and trimming is completed.

Non-symmetry may be developed in a form thrown on two centers, as shown in the work of Robert Fritz. To make such a form, throw a cylinder the size and wall thickness for the completed pot. Move metal plate or plaster bat so that cylinder is off-center. Fasten plate or bat in new position with wads of clay and complete shaping.

TWO CENTERS. 1. Throwing on new center distorts symmetry.

2. Finished form has neck to one side.

Non-symmetry of thrown forms may be emphasized by paddling when leather hard.

Fluting just after throwing by stretching clay from inside with finger develops non-symmetry.

Cast birds of red
earthenware with gray
speckled, semi-matte glaze.
Copper wire comb wattles.

10 · Cast Forms

Clay wares are also formed by the casting process. In this method, liquid clay, which has been specially prepared for the purpose and is known as "casting slip," is poured into a highly absorbent plaster mold.

The dry, porous walls of the mold draw the water out of the clay next to it, causing it to solidify. The clay in the center of the mold, however, remains liquid; and when the clay next to the mold has thickened sufficiently to form a wall, the liquid is poured off, leaving the clay form perfectly fitted to the mold.

This method permits the making of a large number of copies of an original model and is used extensively by pottery manufacturers. It also permits the studio potter to make hollow, thin-walled forms not easily made in other ways.

A simple one-piece mold will provide the best starting place for your experience in making pottery forms by casting. You will need a quantity of potter's plaster and mixing equipment for it (see Chapter 3), a piece of Masonite and linoleum or tar roofing paper strips to make an enclosure to hold the plaster, liquid soap, vaseline or mold soap which you can buy for the purpose of coating any parts of the plaster enclosure which might otherwise stick to the plaster, your ordinary clay and tools, casting slip, and an original model.

Since casting slip is more than a mere dilute mixture of clay and water, it is recommended that you get complete instructions from the supplier of your clay before attempting to make your own slip. Otherwise, you should buy prepared slips from a ceramic supply house. Store slip in a closed, airtight container.

MAKING A ONE-PIECE MOLD

First make the form to be duplicated. It must be one without undercuts, reverse curves or diameter measures greater than that of the top of the piece or it cannot be removed from a one-piece mold. Shallow bowls or wide-mouthed vases can be successfully cast in this type of mold. Make your original shape by any of the methods described thus far in this book and allow it to become leather-hard. It should be smooth and free of bumps, particularly on the outside, as the outside of our model will be

101

duplicated on the inside of your plaster form —which in turn will be the outside surface of the finished cast piece.

Make preparations for casting a mold of your original model by first rolling a clay slab about 2″ thick on a Masonite or linoleum foundation. Use dividers and mark out a circle of the same size as that of the top of the leather-hard clay form. Mark a second circle, using the original center, ½″ larger than the first. Cut along line of outer circle while holding fettling knife tipped so clay edge takes an outward angle and the clay forms a flat, tapered plug. Invert model on plug, fitting rim to line of smaller circle.

Next make an enclosure around assembled plug and model. Use strip of linoleum, tar roofing paper or heavy cardboard and make a cylinder at least 2″ larger all around than the plug and at least 2″ higher than model placed on plug. Tie cylinder at top and bottom with strong cord—tie around middle as well if plaster mold is to be large.

Place cylinder over plug-and-model assembly so margin around it is even, securing cylinder in place with a coil of clay pressed around outside bottom. Seal outside vertical joint with another clay coil. Remove model from the plug temporarily to enable you to seal inside bottom and vertical joint with clay coil; then replace.

Coat inside surfaces of form, including Masonite edge extending beyond clay plug, with soap or vaseline.

Estimate quantities and mix plaster according to directions given in Chapter 3. Pour it into the cylindrical enclosure and over model and plug. Fill to the top with as little splashing as possible—letting plaster flow over fingers at edge of cylinder will break its fall—striving to keep air bubbles out.

When plaster has set undisturbed for an hour, peel away clay coils, cylinder and remove plug and original clay model. Scrape outside edges of mold to remove plaster fins or chips and let it dry in a warm room for at least a week before using.

USING THE MOLD

When your mold is dry, set it on a level surface and pour it full of prepared slip. This should have a consistency like that of heavy table cream. Stand by to add more slip as level of the original pouring sinks. The mold absorbs water from the slip and draws a thickening clay wall against the plaster, and mold must be kept filled with slip until this clay wall is of the desired thickness. Thickness will depend on size and character of the piece being cast but allow clay to form a wall about ¼″ for your first pieces. You will be able to see thickness of the drying layer as it forms next to the plaster.

When wall has attained the desired thickness, pour any clay still liquid from it and invert the mold with its clay lining over heavy wire screen or slats laid over a pan to catch clay drips. Allow to drain for about one-half hour. Then right the mold and scrape and clean rim of the casting with wooden modeling tool. This will help it to dry evenly, without pulling or warping, as piece hardens. As it hardens, it will pull away from the mold to show a parting crack between plaster and clay form. When clay is stiff enough to handle without fear of misshaping, remove it from the mold.

Inclusion of the clay plug will have made a clay margin or collar on your original clay form. When casting is removed from the mold, trim collar away and permit the form to dry until leather-hard. Sponge rim with damp

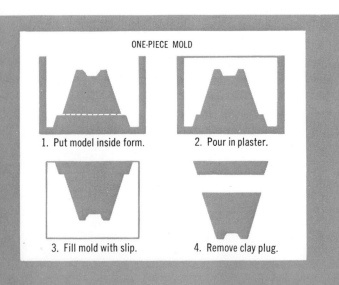

ONE-PIECE MOLD

1. Put model inside form.

2. Pour in plaster.

3. Fill mold with slip.

4. Remove clay plug.

elephant-ear sponge and set it away to dry before biscuit-firing.

THE SOLID CAST ASYMMETRICAL FORM

To make a solid cast asymmetrical form, first model the form which is to form the hollow of the bowl on a piece of Masonite. Model is upside down on the Masonite. When inside form is modeled, draw the proposed outline of the outer edge of the form on the Masonite with an indelible pencil. Build a clay wall ½" thick along the outside mark of penciled line with large coils of plastic clay, making a wall at least ½" higher than the center form. Mix and pour plaster over form to fill space within the clay wall to the top.

As soon as the plaster has set, remove the clay wall and cut and trim the still easily cut plaster to the shape desired for the outside of the bowl or container. There should be no undercut sections on this type of casting form. When plaster is completely hard, smooth it with sandpaper and sponge any loose particles from its surface. Also sponge the Masonite foundation.

Coat plaster model and surrounding Masonite with three coats of soap or vaseline, allowing an interval of about fifteen minutes between each coat. Wipe plaster surface lightly with sponge or soft cloth to remove any excess vaseline or soap. Fasten a tapered plug made of clay, plug to be about 2" long and approximately 1" in diameter at small end, at center of the widest part of bowl bottom.

Next construct an enclosure around the plaster model. This can be a rectangular frame 2" larger on all sides than the model. Make by backing boards with bricks and tying around the board frame with heavy twine. Seal bottom edges inside and out with clay coils; seal at inside corners in a similar manner.

Mix and pour plaster into the enclosure, filling it until ¼" of the clay plug extends above the plaster surface. When plaster has set, remove frame enclosure and turn mold over. Remove the clay mound from the center of the plaster model and cut V-shaped keys on top sides of the mold.

Apply several coats of vaseline or soap to the mold surface, keys and depression left by removal of the clay mound. Sponge or wipe clean as described before.

Reassemble the wooden frame enclosure around the model and pour the second half of the mold. Depth of this will be 2". When plaster is set, separate mold halves and remove clay plug. Let completed mold dry as previously described.

To use the mold, fasten halves of the mold firmly together by tying parts with heavy cord or holding them with several 1" bands of rubber cut from an old inner tube. This mold will serve you in two ways in that it can be used as a drain mold or for making solid castings. Directions for both follow.

THE DRAIN MOLD

This mold is used for drain casting just as described for using the one-piece mold. Fill with slip poured through the hole formed by the plug. Check wall thickness as it forms (continue adding slip as original levels fall) by gently scraping walls of plug. When wall is of desired thickness, invert and drain mold. When clay wall parts from plaster mold, remove mold and trim walls of clay plug from the piece and smooth away any marks left by joint of mold, etc.

To make a solid cast piece with this mold, pour it full of casting slip, continuing to fill it as needed to keep it full at all times until drain hole has filled with a solid plug without a core of liquid clay. The solid cast form will take longer to harden than the drain-cast form. When plug has pulled away from the surrounding plaster, take mold apart and remove the cast form. Sponge with a damp elephant-ear sponge and permit it to dry completely before firing.

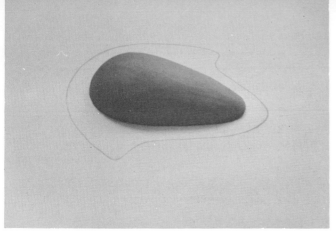

TWO-PIECE MOLD. 1. Make clay mound to form bowl inside; draw outside edge.

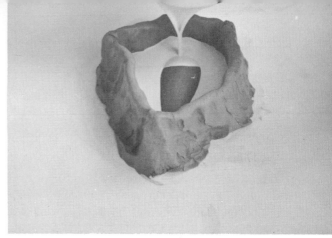

2. Form clay dam around outside line; pour plaster over clay mound.

5. Pour plaster into cylinder, level with end of clay plug. This forms half of mold.

6. Remove mold from form, turn it over, and cut keys into it to lock with other half.

9. Remove model from plaster molds. Note keys for aligning halves of mold.

10. Tape halves of mold together, pour clay slip into drain hole.

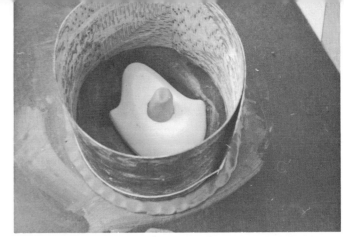

3. Carve and model the plaster casting until it takes desired shape.

4. Add clay plug to plaster model, dress with soap, and place in cylindrical dam.

7. Remove clay mound from mold, replace mold inside dam, and dress with soap.

8. Pour 2 inches of plaster on top of first mold to form second half of two-part mold.

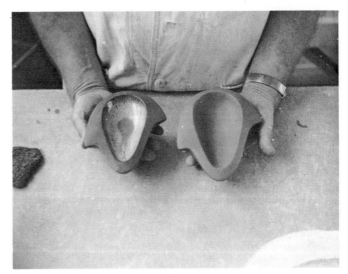

11. Pour excess slip out of mold, let clay dry; then separate halves, trim casting.

12. Smooth and trim cast clay form, then fire. Note shrinkage of form after firing.

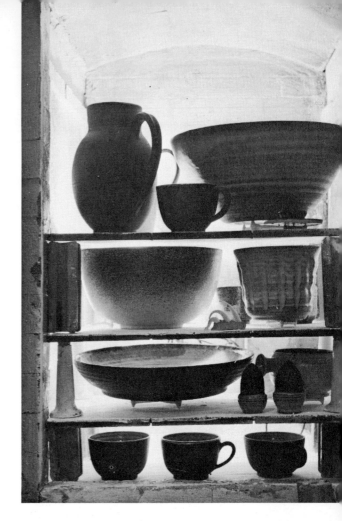

Kiln holds load of glazed pieces. Note cones.

11 · Firing the Kiln

Few craft experiences give more satisfaction than taking perfectly fired ware from the kiln. It is a satisfaction not dulled by the occasional piece which is, for one reason or another, somewhat less than perfect. The firing process is the test of your skill as a craftsman in the building of the ware, just as it is firing that makes a dried clay shape become a durable form.

If you are a beginner, working at home or in a class, your first pieces will probably be fired in a kiln operated by someone else. You will, however, be interested in knowing something of kilns and how they are fired as you may well own and operate a kiln eventually, even as a hobbyist.

KINDS OF KILNS

Kilns are of several kinds and may be referred to according to features such as fuel used, the operating phases, such as "periodic" or "continuous," or as being of the "open" or "muffle" variety.

In the home, schools or studios, the kiln will be a periodic one—stacked with ware, fired to maturing point for the ware, cooled, drawn, and again stacked, fired, etc. The continuous kiln, kept in constant operation over long periods of time, is used industrially. The open kiln is also largely industrial. In this type, flames and smoke circulate through the firing chamber and ware being fired is protected from direct effects of flame and smoke by being placed in especially constructed fire clay boxes. These boxes are known as "saggars." Just as an experiment, you might put a small pinch-formed pot under a flower pot and put it in the fireplace at some time when you plan to have a fire there for several hours. Since no temperature control is possible, this is far from being a scientific experiment, but it demonstrates the seeming miracle of ceramics—the turning of clay into a permanent structure by fire.

In the muffle kiln, the ware is protected from smoke, flames and fumes by the muffle which surrounds the firing chamber. In this kiln the ware is stacked on shelves made of fire clay and is heated by radiation from the muffle wall. Present-day muffle kilns use oil or gas as fuel and are most commonly used in schools and studios.

The electric kiln provides the cleanest possible firing conditions and a muffle or saggars are not needed since flames, etc., are absent. Heat is provided by radiation from several types of electric elements such as Nichrome wire and Nichrome ribbon, both of which are nickel chromium alloys; the Globar, which is a carborundum rod; and the Swedish Kanthol element, the composition of which is unknown.

The small electric kiln with a Nichrome element is recommended for home use. It will take less "house room" than most household appliances, can be plugged into the ordinary wall socket and, because it is small, firings can be frequent and firing periods relatively short. Temperatures to be obtained in kilns to operate on ordinary house wiring circuits are necessarily lower than those to be had under other conditions, but they will prove adequate for many clays and glazes customarily used in the practice of ceramics as a hobby.

KILN FURNITURE

The interior of the unloaded kiln is a bare, open area and you will need a few pieces of kiln furniture before the space can be effi-ciently filled with ware. This furniture consists of slabs made of fireclay, posts of varying heights and sizes to support the slabs and thus form interior shelves in the kiln, and various stilts, pins and buttons to hold glazed pieces up and away from direct contact with shelves or kiln bottom. How many shelves, posts or stilts you will need depends on kiln size and type of load, naturally. When purchasing even a small electric test kiln, it will be well to acquire at least one shelf and four supporting posts, plus a few stilts and pins. All of these will be available at your ceramic supply dealer's.

STACKING THE KILN

Really efficient loading or stacking of the kiln may take practice. For economy of operation and most even heat distribution in the firing chamber, put as many pieces in it as you can. Do keep these things in mind, however: leave at least ½" open space between shelf edges and muffle wall or electric elements; leave at least ½" space between walls and ware and from ¼" to ½" space between all pieces of glazed ware. Green ware, without glaze, can touch. Small bowls or cups can be placed directly in larger bowls, and the cup hold a handful of beads or buttons for this first, or biscuit-fire. It will be wise to avoid placing a very heavy, although not particularly large, piece on one with thin walls.

If you have pieces custom-fired, you will find that the biscuit-firing of a single piece will cost less than having the same piece glost-fired. The foregoing makes the reasons for this obvious. Other considerations which must be taken into account in the firing of glazed wares follow.

As said before, glazed pieces mustn't be allowed to touch in the firing. As it becomes molten, the glaze may swell and bubble out from the glazed surface. Moreover, glazes will fuse to make "Siamese twins" of separate, but touching, pieces to the ruination, usually, of both. Another point to note in the handling and stacking of glazed ware is the necessity of supporting the pieces on the stilts, pins and buttons required to keep them up from shelf surfaces or the bottom of the firing chamber. Glaze fuses to shelves, too, if it runs from the sides of the piece and drips on them. In glost-firing, shelves should be further protected from stray glaze drips by a coating of "kiln wash" painted on with a brush. Buy the wash as a powder and mix it with water to a thin paste and apply a generous coat or two for safety. Lifting any glaze drips will pull wash loose but chipped wash is easily patched.

PYROMETRIC CONES

In all firing, biscuit or glost, the ceramist makes use of pyrometric cones. These are slender, trihedral (a figure defined by three planes meeting at a point) pyramids made of a mixture of ceramic materials graded to accord with a progressive series of fusion points. They are numbered from 022, the lowest of the series, through 021, 020, and so on, up ("up" as regards temperature indications although figures become lower) until 01 is reached. There is no Cone 0, but the series then continues as Cone 1, 2, 3, etc., up to 42. This is the last of the series and represents a temperature far exceeding the needs of the average potter.

A glance at the accompanying table will show a figure indicating a corresponding temperature reading opposite that indicating a number of a pyrometric cone. It should be understood, however, that cones do not measure temperature. Instead, they measure the amount of heat-work done within the kiln up to the time of their melting and consequent deformation. When the pyramid tip of the cone collapses (with the heat, so to speak), it means that clays and glazes which required a certain time-temperature relationship to mature have done so.

Pyrometric cones are necessary because of the time-temperature relationship spoken of above. If you have ever boiled an egg, you will know that you can bring it to the same degree of hardness by simmering it several minutes in water over a low fire, or by rapidly bringing the water to a galloping boil over a high flame. The size of the pan, the number of eggs, the amount of water—all these are factors that count in arriving at a breakfast egg of just that degree of hardness that you desire. So it is in the kiln. A slow, gradual heating of the ware will bring it to maturity at a lower temperature than would be the case if heating was rapid. A large, and completely loaded, kiln will take longer to reach a certain temperature than a small one holding only a few pieces. A peek into the kiln to see how the cones are reacting to the conditions existing in the kiln reveals important clues.

Pyrometric cones are usually set in the kiln in series of three. They must be made to stand up by inserting them in a small rectangular wad of clay. There must be a "spy hole" in the kiln to allow observation of the cones during firing, and they must be placed on shelf or post so they can be seen from the spy hole. Large kilns have more than one spy hole, usually one at front and back; small kilns have hole in the front only. A series of cones may be placed at several vantage points in a large kiln as parts of it may become hotter than others and consequent allowances must be made.

To enlarge on the foregoing points, let us say that you will fire to Cone 06. Many clays and glazes are adequately matured at this cone and it falls within temperature range possible to achieve in a small electric kiln. Purchase standard size cones in numbers 05, 06 and 07. This last will respond to the effects of time and temperature first. It is the "warning" cone, and the melting and curling over of its tip indicates that the kiln's contents are approaching maturity. This cone is set into the clay rectangle at the angle shown in the diagram and at the right-hand end of it. Cone 06, the curling of which indicates maturity of the ware and announces that the fire should be turned off, is set at the center. The left-hand cone, Number 05, is the "guard" cone, and should not become deformed if heat is withdrawn at the proper time.

Make up several cone plaques at a time if you consistently fire to the same cone—a good idea for the beginner—and allow clay bases to get completely and thoroughly dry before using. The clay should include some grog to reduce its shrinkage. If, during drying and firing, clay support shrinks less than the cones, they may loosen and fall out. If it shrinks more than cones, it may break cones off at the base. If all this sounds complicated, although it is really quite simple, buy some cone holders from the ceramics supply house.

FIRING

When kiln is stacked and cones placed so they can be viewed from the spy hole during firing,

heating of the kiln can begin. Do not close the kiln completely right at first. Although ware seemed perfectly dry when put in the kiln, green clay and fresh glazes hold "chemical water" and this moisture must be driven off as steam and the steam must escape from the firing chamber. Leave peep hole uncovered or door ajar until interior of the kiln is rosy red.

Kilns with fuel controls will have the controls turned up from time to time during the firing. The small electric kiln usually has no controls other than "on " and "off"—and simply gets hotter as time goes on. To start such a kiln it is only necessary to plug it in. When the first cone deforms, stand by to be ready to turn kiln off when the middle cone is down. Do not, under any circumstances, open the door of any kiln, until it is completely cool. The resulting cold shock to the hot ware may cause it to crack or shatter—a danger not only to the contents of the kiln but to you.

Most gas-fired muffle type kilns have pilot lights in addition to the burners. The proper

CONE AND COMPARATIVE TEMPERATURE CHART

Cone Number	When fired slowly 68°F. per hour Fahrenheit	When fired rapidly 302°F. per hour Fahrenheit	Cone Number	When fired slowly 68°F. per hour Fahrenheit	When fired rapidly 302°F. per hour Fahrenheit
022	1085	1121	06	1841	1859
021	1103	1139	05	1886	1904
020	1157	1202	04	1922	1940
019	1166	1220	03	1976	2039
018	1238	1328	02	2003	2057
017	1328	1418	01	2030	2093
016	1355	1463	1	2057	2120
015	1418	1481	2	2075	2129
014	1463	1526	3	2093	2138
013	1517	1580	4	2129	2174
012	1544	1607	5	2156	2201
011	1607	1661	6	2174	2246
010	1634	1643	7	2210	2282
09	1706	1706	8	2237	2300
08	1733	1742	9	2282	2345
07	1787	1814			

procedure in starting such a kiln is to turn on the pilots one at a time, lighting each from underneath the kiln or with a torch inserted in the firebox. When pilots are lit, burners are turned on low, one at a time until all are operating; then pilots are turned off. If necessary, turn up burners every two or three hours until desired cone has deformed. Adjust burners to a clean blue flame throughout the firing. A yellow flame indicates that the mixture lacks sufficient air and this may cause blistering of glazes or a condition within the kiln known as "reduction" which affects glaze colors. Excessive gas may also cause glaze defects, such as sulfuring or scumming.

Each kiln has a temperament and personality of its own. You can learn how to get the best results from a particular kiln only by experimenting with it. Size and type, as well as kind and size of load and fuels, determine how long it will take to bring any kiln load to maturity. The small electric test kiln holding few pieces may need only two or three hours to reach the desired heat. If the electric kiln is larger, and equipped with switch allowing heat to be turned on low, medium and high, it would probably be heated at low for one or two hours, at medium for a similar length of time, and then turned on high until firing was completed, then turned off immediately.

Take particular care in firing with gas and such combustible fuels. Should gas burners go out at any time during the firing, turn off all gas and wait a day before relighting pilots or burners.

Before purchasing any kiln, gas or electric, be sure that it is constructed to fire safely at temperatures you want to reach. In other words, if you want to use cones that call for temperatures above 2000 F., check specifications for the kiln to see if linings and elements are designed to withstand this heat without damage. Kilns last longer if consistently fired at less than the stated maximum temperatures. Electric elements burn out in time but are replaceable.

OXIDATION AND REDUCTION FIRING

The above discussion of firing emphasizes oxidation, where there is more oxygen in the ware chamber than is needed for the body and glaze to remain in their normal condition as oxides of the various elements. The atmosphere for oxidation firing is composed primarily of carbon dioxide plus oxygen.

The next type of firing is the Oriental middle fire, or what we call neutral fire, where there is just sufficient oxygen in the ware chamber to form carbon dioxide.

The third type is reduction firing, where the atmosphere is composed of carbon dioxide plus carbon. The free carbon is greedy for oxygen and robs the coloring oxides of a part or all of their oxygen, causing a color change.

Low-temperature glaze materials, particularly the lead compounds, are less stable than the materials used in glazes from cone 5 to cone 10, therefore reduction at lower temperatures is seldom desirable and may result in blistered glazes. Reduction at high temperatures may cause a subtle change in textural quality of the glaze and increased richness as well as a change in color. True reduction firing requires an open-type kiln, either updraft or downdraft. Don't attempt reduction in your electric or muffle kiln unless you are quite experienced and there are no fire hazards.

Unfired and fired pyrometric cones

Home-made potter's wheel
has optional elbow rest.

12 · Building a Potter's Wheel

Many potters prefer an electrically driven wheel. However, most wheels of this type have the disadvantage of running at a constant speed—a handicap to the beginner who needs control of speed at all times. Variable speed motors are available, but they are expensive, The home-assembled wheel illustrated here gives speed control with a $\frac{1}{4}$-horsepower motor (quite inexpensive). The motor operates the wheel by friction drive.

The motor and a foot pedal are mounted on a hinged shelf underneath the bench. A rubber-tired wheel on the motor shaft presses against a large disc, which serves as a fly-wheel to turn the potter's wheel. The assembly requires a metal shaft and bearings, two plywood discs, and a sturdy wooden frame to house the operating unit.

Pick up the metal parts at a machine shop or a junk yard. You'll need some help from a machinist in fitting the shaft into the bearings, unless you can find parts that already fit, or unless you have a lathe and metal working equipment of your own. Make the shaft of any straight piece of metal that can be machined. (It should be at least 1″ in diameter.) Use an automobile axle if you find bearings to fit it. If you have the shaft turned by a machinist, use a piece of steel that is slightly softer than that in an auto axle.

You can buy bearings wherever used auto and appliance parts are sold. Use a crankshaft bearing where the shaft connects with wheel head. Any type of thrust bearing may be used at the bottom where shaft attaches to flywheel.

Both the 12″ wheel and the 28″ disc for the flywheel in this assembly were made of ¾″ plywood. (Use marine plywood and paint each side with linseed oil to waterproof and prevent warping.)

To make the flywheel sufficiently heavy, weight it with an old flat-belt pulley 18″ in diameter. Drill holes through spokes of the pulley wheel so it can be bolted to the underside of the disc. Since the wheel is powered by friction drive, no belts are required. The flywheel can be used also as a kick wheel. Some potters may prefer a heavier wheel. If you do, attach a larger flat-belt pulley to the plywood disc and fill in the spaces between spokes with cement.

The hinged shelf on which the motor is mounted is held up away from the flywheel disc by a short expansion spring. The foot pedal is mounted at the right front edge of the shelf. Pressure on the pedal against the spring permits the shelf to drop. The rubber-tired wheel on the motor shaft presses against the plywood disc and turns it. The amount of pressure applied to the pedal determines wheel speed.

The small drive wheel should have a setscrew so you can fit it onto the motor shaft yourself. Or, have a machinist mount the small wheel for you. On this motor drive wheel, use a rubber tire designed for model autos, available at hobby shops. Add a friction brake, as shown, if you wish, holding it up with a screen door spring. You can stop the wheel as you like with foot pressure.

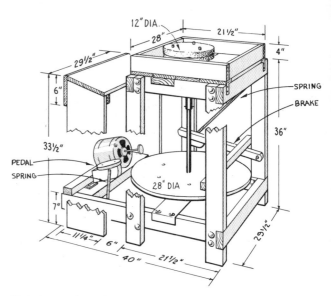

Note two springs. One holds motor drive up off flywheel, other holds up brake shoe.

Two by fours were used for the wooden frame and were joined with lap and half-lap joints and fastened with two machine bolts and two metal washers at each joint. The dimensions can vary. Make the height and distance between table and bench to suit yourself. The bench seat is built on an incline to help you lean toward your work.

You can buy plaster bats or cast your own to use on top of the wheel head. Use the aluminum discs which come in some craft woodworking equipment. They are held on the wheel head by three pegs.

If you'd rather not bother hunting parts for your wheel, and don't mind the extra expense, you may be able to buy a shaft, two sets of steel ball bearings, an aluminum head, and a cast iron flywheel to assemble into a home-built frame. It is also possible to buy a throwing head set with a ¾″ bore. Check hobby shops or surplus stores in your area, or try such sources that sell mail order. Mail order scientific instrument suppliers are another possible source.

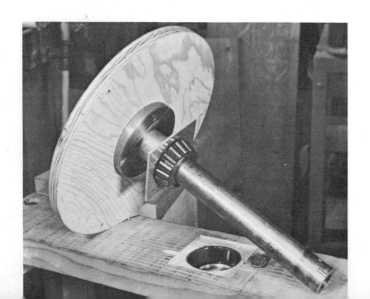

Underside of potter's wheel. Note automotive-type bearing used here.